Related Books of Interest

W9-BXX-138

Patterns of Information Management

By Mandy Chessell and Harald C. Smith
ISBN: 978-0-13-315550-1

Use Best Practice Patterns to Understand and Architect Manageable, Efficient Information Supply Chains That Help You Leverage All Your Data and Knowledge

Building on the analogy of a supply chain, Mandy Chessell and Harald Smith explain how information can be transformed, enriched, reconciled, redistributed, and utilized in even the most complex environments. Through a realistic, end-to-end case study, they help you blend overlapping information management, SOA, and BPM technologies that are often viewed as competitive.

Using this book's patterns, you can integrate all levels of your architecture—from holistic, enterprise, system-level views down to low-level design elements. You can fully address key non-functional requirements such as the amount, quality, and pace of incoming data. Above all, you can create an IT landscape that is coherent, interconnected, efficient, effective, and manageable.

The Business of IT
How to Improve Service and Lower Costs

By Robert Ryan and Tim Raducha-Grace
ISBN: 978-0-13-700061-6

Drive More Business Value from IT…and Bridge the Gap Between IT and Business Leadership

IT organizations have achieved outstanding technological maturity, but many have been slower to adopt world-class business practices. This book provides IT and business executives with methods to achieve greater business discipline throughout IT, collaborate more effectively, sharpen focus on the customer, and drive greater value from IT investment. Drawing on their experience consulting with leading IT organizations, Robert Ryan and Tim Raducha-Grace help IT leaders make sense of alternative ways to improve IT service and lower cost, including ITIL, IT financial management, balanced scorecards, and business cases. You'll learn how to choose the best approaches to improve IT business practices for your environment and use these practices to improve service quality, reduce costs, and drive top-line revenue growth.

Sign up for the monthly IBM Press newsletter at ibmpressbooks/newsletters

Related Books of Interest

The Art of Enterprise Information Architecture

A Systems-Based Approach for Unlocking Business Insight

By Mario Godinez, Eberhard Hechler, Klaus Koenig, Steve Lockwood, Martin Oberhofer, and Michael Schroeck
ISBN: 978-0-13-703571-7

Architecture for the Intelligent Enterprise: Powerful New Ways to Maximize the Real-Time Value of Information

Tomorrow's winning "Intelligent Enterprises" will bring together far more diverse sources of data, analyze it in more powerful ways, and deliver immediate insight to decision-makers throughout the organization. Today, however, most companies fail to apply the information they already have, while struggling with the complexity and costs of their existing information environments.

In this book, a team of IBM's leading information management experts guide you on a journey that will take you from where you are today toward becoming an "Intelligent Enterprise."

The New Era of Enterprise Business Intelligence:

Using Analytics to Achieve a Global Competitive Advantage

By Mike Biere
ISBN: 978-0-13-707542-3

A Complete Blueprint for Maximizing the Value of Business Intelligence in the Enterprise

The typical enterprise recognizes the immense potential of business intelligence (BI) and its impact upon many facets within the organization—but it's not easy to transform BI's potential into real business value. Top BI expert Mike Biere presents a complete blueprint for creating winning BI strategies and infrastructure and systematically maximizing the value of information throughout the enterprise.

This product-independent guide brings together start-to-finish guidance and practical checklists for every senior IT executive, planner, strategist, implementer, and the actual business users themselves.

 Listen to the author's podcast at:
ibmpressbooks.com/podcasts

Visit ibmpressbooks.com
for all product information

Related Books of Interest

Enterprise Master Data Management
An SOA Approach to Managing Core Information

By Allen Dreibelbis, Eberhard Hechler, Ivan Milman, Martin Oberhofer, Paul Van Run, and Dan Wolfson
ISBN: 978-0-13-236625-0

The Only Complete Technical Primer for MDM Planners, Architects, and Implementers

Enterprise Master Data Management provides an authoritative, vendor-independent MDM technical reference for practitioners: architects, technical analysts, consultants, solution designers, and senior IT decision makers. Written by the IBM® data management innovators who are pioneering MDM, this book systematically introduces MDM's key concepts and technical themes, explains its business case, and illuminates how it interrelates with and enables SOA.

Drawing on their experience with cutting-edge projects, the authors introduce MDM patterns, blueprints, solutions, and best practices published nowhere else—everything you need to establish a consistent, manageable set of master data, and use it for competitive advantage.

Mining the Talk
Unlocking the Business Value in Unstructured Information
Spangler, Kreulen
ISBN: 978-0-13-233953-7

Decision Management Systems
A Practical Guide to Using Business Rules and Predictive Analytics
Taylor
ISBN: 978-0-13-288438-9

IBM Cognos Business Intelligence v10
The Complete Guide
Gautam
ISBN: 978-0-13-272472-2

IBM Cognos 10 Report Studio
Practical Examples
Draskovic, Johnson
ISBN: 978-0-13-265675-7

Data Integration Blueprint and Modeling
Techniques for a Scalable and Sustainable Architecture
Giordano
ISBN: 978-0-13-708493-7

Sign up for the monthly IBM Press newsletter at ibmpressbooks/newsletters

Praise for *Analytics Across the Enterprise*

"Few major high-tech companies eat their own dog food. But give IBM credit: It practices what it preaches. This book provides an inside look at how IBM has applied analytics to nine business functions, the lessons it has learned, and the value it has derived. This book is valuable for anyone in a large company who wants to know how to apply analytics profitably."

—**Wayne Eckerson**, Principal Consultant, Eckerson Group, and author, *Secrets of Analytical Leaders: Insights from Information Insiders*

"*Analytics Across the Enterprise* shows how even the most complex enterprise can transform itself with analytics. A powerful collection of real-world projects shows that using analytics to improve decisions, especially operational decisions, drives efficiency *and* innovation. The stories in this very readable book show the importance of actually taking action, not just developing insight; of caring about the end user context, not just the model; of gaining buy-in and managing organizational change; and much more. A great guide for anyone transforming their own organization with analytics."

—**James Taylor**, author, *Decision Management Systems: A Practical Guide to Using Business Rules and Predictive Analytics* (IBM Press)

"*Analytics Across the Enterprise* is the only book on analytics written by three world-class experts 'standing on the shoulders of a giant' analytics powerhouse: an impressive first-hand account of nine breakthrough analytic journeys from 70 top executives and practitioners, the largest private math department in the world, and a leading consulting think tank. This is an unprecedented tour de force showing how a best-of-breed analytics company revolutionized its own business model."

—**Gonçalo Pacheco de Almeida**, Associate Professor of Strategy, Head of the Business Analytics Initiative, and Academic Director of the MBA Strategy Specialization, HEC Paris Business School and the French National Scientific Research Center–HEC Lab

"A thoughtfully written collection of stories from within IBM, with proven techniques that are valuable for all current and future business leaders. IBM has been doing analytics since before it was 'cool' and, for the first time, shares an inside look at the very pragmatic, inspiring approach complete with lessons learned. *Analytics Across the Enterprise* not only changes the game, it explains how to win."

—**Lawrence G. Singleton**, PhD, CPA, Dean, School of Management, Professor of Accounting and International Business, Marist College

"Organizations are awash in data. Many have transformed this data into information, yet few have identified patterns of insight from this information. A rare number of organizations can take the insight to action, but even fewer can create a pathway from data to decisions. In *Analytics Across the Enterprise,* Dietrich, Plachy, and Norton definitively chronicle what it takes to apply big data and analytics in the transformation of enterprises. The results: Successful leaders create competitive advantage in smarter workforces, optimized supply chains, and predictable sales performance. Organizations will learn how to move not only from gut-feel intuition but also to powerful fact-based decision making."

—**R "Ray" Wang**, Principal Analyst and Founder, Constellation Research, Inc.

"The growing demand for analytics is a priority for business and IT to collaborate on the processes and technology required to gain the insights to guide organizations to be effective. This book helps organizations gain a perspective on what operating analytics across the enterprise is all about and most importantly why it is crucial across lines of business where the outcomes can be achieved from making continuous investments."

—**Mark Smith**, CEO and Chief Research Officer, Ventana Research

"Glimpses of the IBM vision of the future for analytics have regularly appeared in the literature, and now for the first time we have a comprehensive inside account of how IBM uses advanced analytics to compete globally. Using examples from many functions (HR, marketing, finance, supply chain), this book provides a fascinating view of IBM as an intensively data-driven corporation. Senior executives familiar with analytics and data applications will find many ideas in this book on how they can harness analytics to improve their corporation's performance. Executives less familiar with analytics may experience some 'shock and awe' in reading how far data- and analytics-driven corporations have progressed and what formidable competitors they have become."

—**Peter C. Bell**, Professor, Management Science, Ivey Business School at Western University

"*Analytics Across the Enterprise* is a live chronicle of how the practice of analytics transcends the business functional boundaries and how it benefits all the business functions."

—**Dr. Adam Fadlalla**, Associate Dean for Academic Affairs and Professor of Information Systems, College of Business and Economics, Qatar University

"The use of data and analytics to generate value is a journey for all organizations: a journey of technology, operational self-awareness, and culture. The joy and challenge of data and analytics is that it is difficult, and as such, it is a source of sustainable competitive value. This book tells the story of the journey of adoption of analytics for IBM and how we became a company driven by data and analytics. It explores the technical and mathematical complexities of the journey, the different business use cases, and the value it delivered to our clients, our employees, and our shareholders."

—**Fred Balboni**, Global Managing Partner, Strategy and Analytics, Global Business Services, IBM Corporation

Analytics Across the Enterprise

Analytics Across the Enterprise

How IBM Realizes Business Value from Big Data and Analytics

Brenda L. Dietrich, Emily C. Plachy,
and Maureen F. Norton

IBM Press
Pearson plc

Upper Saddle River, NJ • Boston • Indianapolis • San Francisco
New York • Toronto • Montreal • London • Munich • Paris • Madrid
Cape Town • Sydney • Tokyo • Singapore • Mexico City
ibmpressbooks.com

The authors and publisher have taken care in the preparation of this book, but make no expressed or implied warranty of any kind and assume no responsibility for errors or omissions. No liability is assumed for incidental or consequential damages in connection with or arising out of the use of the information or programs contained herein.

© Copyright 2014 by International Business Machines Corporation. All rights reserved.

Note to U.S. Government Users: Documentation related to restricted right. Use, duplication, or disclosure is subject to restrictions set forth in GSA ADP Schedule Contract with IBM Corporation.

IBM Press Program Managers: Steven M. Stansel, Ellice Uffer
Cover design: IBM Corporation
Associate Publisher: Dave Dusthimer
Marketing Manager: Stephane Nakib
Executive Editor: Mary Beth Ray
Publicist: Heather Fox
Development Editor: Allison Beaumont Johnson
Technical Editors: John Lucas, Ken Sloan
Managing Editor: Kristy Hart
Designer: Alan Clements
Senior Project Editor: Betsy Gratner
Copy Editor: Kitty Wilson
Indexer: WordWise Publishing Services
Compositor: Nonie Ratcliff
Proofreader: Debbie Williams
Manufacturing Buyer: Dan Uhrig

Published by Pearson plc

Publishing as IBM Press

For information about buying this title in bulk quantities, or for special sales opportunities (which may include electronic versions; custom cover designs; and content particular to your business, training goals, marketing focus, or branding interests), please contact our corporate sales department at corpsales@pearsoned.com or (800) 382-3419.

For government sales inquiries, please contact governmentsales@pearsoned.com.

For questions about sales outside the U.S., please contact international@pearsoned.com.

The following terms are trademarks of International Business Machines Corporation in many jurisdictions worldwide: IBM, IBM Press, IBM Watson, Global Business Services, Smarter Planet, Smarter Commerce, System p, Cognos, TM1, SPSS, QRadar, Q1 Labs, IBM Social Business, Smarter Cities, PureSystems, ILOG, WebSphere, DB2, Global Technology Services, and DemandTec. Kenexa is a registered trademark of Kenexa, an IBM Company. Other product and service names might be trademarks of IBM or other companies. A current list of IBM trademarks is available on the Web at www.ibm.com/legal/copytrade.shtml.

UNIX is a registered trademark of The Open Group in the United States and other countries. Intel, Intel logo, Intel Inside, Intel Inside logo, Intel Centrino, Intel Centrino logo, Celeron, Intel Xeon, Intel SpeedStep, Itanium, and Pentium are trademarks or registered trademarks of Intel Corporation or its subsidiaries in the United States and other countries. Other company, product, or service names may be trademarks or service marks of others.

Library of Congress Control Number: 2014934177

All rights reserved. This publication is protected by copyright, and permission must be obtained from the publisher prior to any prohibited reproduction, storage in a retrieval system, or transmission in any form or by any means, electronic, mechanical, photocopying, recording, or likewise. For information regarding permissions, write to:

Pearson Education, Inc.
Rights and Contracts Department
501 Boylston Street, Suite 900
Boston, MA 02116
Fax (617) 671-3447

ISBN-13: 978-0-13-383303-4
ISBN-10: 0-13-383303-8

Text printed in the United States on recycled paper at R.R. Donnelley in Crawfordsville, Indiana.
Second Printing: August 2014

For the many pioneers at IBM who are breaking new ground
to realize business value from big data and analytics.

Contents

xiii

Foreword

Like many of our clients, IBM® itself is focused on becoming a smarter enterprise. Connected people, integrated processes, and instrumented data: These form the foundation for "smarter." A smarter enterprise makes decisions differently, creates value differently, and delivers value differently...and it all starts with the creative application of analytics.

In my conversations with clients about transformation, they often ask how IBM has approached analytics. Where should we get started? What are you doing inside IBM? What advice would you offer from your experience so far?

To help answer these questions for clients, our analytics practitioners inside IBM collaborated to develop this book. IBM has moved aggressively the past several years to build our analytics capabilities—through hiring talent, developing software, and acquiring firms with analytics tools that enhance our portfolio. IBM itself has been the alpha and beta for the deployment of these new technologies across our operations—from how we manage finance and marketing to how we optimize our supply chain and attract, retain, and develop talent. Indeed, we've found that in virtually every aspect of your organization, you can make smarter, more informed decisions by embedding analytics into how you do business.

I hope you will find our experience relevant and useful as you consider how to best seize on the power of big data, the world's newest natural resource for competitive advantage. Progressive leaders are putting big data to work in fields ranging from finance to farming, from presidential politics to professional sports. It's not just the data; it's the insights gained from analyzing data that give organizations an edge over the competition.

As I tell clients, transformation is hard; it takes ongoing commitment and leadership from the top of the organization. But if there's one truth I've learned about transformation over the years, it's that you should always move faster than you think you should. That's the only way to stay ahead of today's unrelenting pace of change.

This principle holds true for the adoption of analytics, the centerpiece of the next wave of our transformation. Don't wait for your data to be perfect. The time to start on this journey is now...and we hope our own experience at IBM will help you accelerate the benefits that accrue when you unlock the hidden value and power of your data.

—Linda Sanford

IBM Senior Vice President, Enterprise Transformation

Preface

The genesis for this book came when Doug Dow, Vice President, Business Analytics Transformation, observed that a number of good analytics books were being published, written by experts in analytics, and that IBM had experts with significant experience solving business problems by applying analytics. Dow approached Brenda Dietrich, an IBM Fellow and an eminent operations research and analytics expert. Dietrich was receptive to the idea but was reluctant to sign up to write the book alone. Dow later approached two of his Business Analytics Transformation department members, Emily Plachy and Maureen Norton, who both jumped at the chance to tell IBM's story. Another motivation for the book is that Dow receives frequent requests from clients to learn how IBM is using analytics to elevate business results, so we know that IBM's story is of interest.

As we embarked on the journey to write this book about analytics, we were mindful of the rising tide of materials touting the value of analytics. So what would cause someone to cast his or her net and catch this one? Would a book about the challenges and triumphs, to continue the analogy, of one of the largest global ships on the sea have insights and lessons that others could benefit from, or at least find entertaining enough to read? We decided that this is a story that needed to be told. We decided that C-level executives in Fortune 500 companies, small business owners, and MBA students and faculty would see themselves and their challenges on these pages, and we needed to write this book. Introducing readers to a wide spectrum of ideas about how analytics is much more than a technology and instead is a smarter way of doing business would be reason enough to sail forward.

When we started planning for the book, we decided to organize it by business function. We identified analytics projects within a business function that were realizing value. Next, we interviewed the key members on the projects. Then, one of the authors volunteered to be the lead writer for that chapter.

We authors made heavy use of IBM Connections, IBM's collaborative software, to interact as we wrote the book, creating a Connections Activity for the book, organized by chapters. During reviews, we added Connections Folders and Files, which helped us keep track of the many reviews and versions of each chapter. With three authors working in different locations, efficient collaboration was essential.

As the writing journey progressed, a common phrase kept coming into our conversations: "All roads lead to the book." The book became a seminal part of our work, feeding and enriching every aspect of our day jobs. We were able to leverage insights from the work to improve insights and results, effect connections between teams that were tackling similar problems, and help other transformation teams tell their stories.

Another very exciting aspect to this book is that we wanted it to be useful to the business leaders of today and tomorrow; reaching students and faculty is a high priority. During the development of the book, two of the authors, Maureen and Emily, developed and taught an innovative three-day pilot workshop at a premier MBA program in Europe, HEC University. Working with Dr. Hammou Messatfa, Technical Leader, European Government Industry, IBM Sales and Distribution, they held a very successful big data and analytics workshop, which led to additional analytic educational initiatives. Just as the book was in the final editing stages, Maureen had the opportunity to teach at a big data and analytics workshop for MBA students in the Middle East as well.

Color Images

PDFs of the color images for this book can be downloaded from the companion website. Go to www.ibmpressbooks.com/title/9780133833034 and click the Downloads tab.

Acknowledgments

The stories in this book, detailing IBM's use of analytics to transform processes and results, could not have been told without the time, talent, and cooperation of many people. Some have been quoted in the chapters or referenced in endnotes, but many more helped along the way. We thank Ross Mauri and Doug Dow, whose enthusiasm and executive support of this project made it possible. We interviewed more than 70 people, including executives and practitioners, and we worked with staff members, communications professionals, editors, and more from the teams. We are very grateful to the people mentioned below for telling us their stories and contributing to this book.

Foreword: Linda Sanford, Tim Ensign

Chapter 1: Doug Dow, Jeff Jonas, Ross Mauri

Chapter 2: Murray Campbell, Rafi Ezry, Jonathan Ferrar, Werner Geyer, Vlad Gogish, Rudy Karsan, Zahir Ladhani, Stela Lupushor, Randy MacDonald, Sadat Shami

Chapter 3: Naoki Abe, Steve Bayline, Mila Davidzenka, Markus Ettl, Mark Evancho, Donnie Haye, Renee Hook, Pat Knight, Rahul Nahar, Fran O'Sullivan, John Wargo, Emmanuel Yashchin, Paul Zulpa

Chapter 4: Mike Billmeier, Peter Hayes, Carlos Passi, Paul Price, Christian Toft-Nielsen, Natalia Ruderman

Chapter 5: James Correa, Suzy Deffeyes, Matthew Ganis, Jeanette Horan, Francoise Legoues, George Stark, Marie Wallace, Sara Weber

Chapter 6: Melody Dunn, Ben Edwards, Stefanos Manganaris, Stephen Scott, Chris Wong

Chapter 7: Jean Francois Abramatic, Nick Kadochnikov

Chapter 8: Mark Allman, Robert Baseman, Soumyadip Ghosh, Pierre Haren, Perry Hartswick, Jean Francois Puget, Peter Rimshnick, Harley Witt

Chapter 9: David Bush, Matt Callahan, Martin Fleming, Nicholas Otto, Stephen Piper, Kylie Skeahan, Patricia Spugani

Chapter 10: Cesar Berrospi, Jack Bisceglia, Odellia Boni, Greg Dillon, Daniel D'Elena, Sherif Goma, Joe Haugsland, Abdel Labbi, Sergey Makogon, Gregory Westerwick, James Williams

In addition to these people, several others added to the stories in meaningful ways during their review: Jonathan Correnti, Patrick Gibney, Mark Harris, and Ruth Manners. Greg Golden provided valuable guidance and support to get us started. We would also like to thank Steven Stansel and Ellice Uffer from IBM Press for their early encouragement and ongoing support and Mary Beth Ray and the many others from Pearson Education who improved the book and brought it over the finish line. We would like to thank Doug Dow, who read each chapter numerous times, providing valuable feedback. Each of us also owes a debt of gratitude to our families. Writing this book involved many nights, weekends, holidays, and "vacations." Brenda is grateful for the support and uninterrupted writing time that Peter, Joshua, Monica, Ingrid, and Irwin accommodated. Emily treasures the support and keen interest in "the book," as well as the detailed, constructive feedback for one of the chapters, she received from her husband, Tony. Maureen cherishes the inspiration and enthusiastic support for "the book" she received from her husband, Bill, and their three children, Erin, Colleen, and William. Each of us now understands why so many authors apologize to their families in the acknowledgments section.

About the Authors

Dr. Brenda L. Dietrich is an IBM Fellow and Vice President. She joined IBM in 1984 and has worked in the area now called analytics for her entire career. Her early work involved applying mathematical models to improve the performance of IBM manufacturing lines. During her career, she has worked with almost every IBM business unit and applied analytics to numerous IBM decision processes. For more than a decade, she led the Mathematical Sciences function in the IBM Research division, where she was responsible for both basic research on computational mathematics and for the development of novel applications of mathematics for both IBM and its clients. In addition to her work within IBM, she has been the president of INFORMS, the world's largest professional society for operations research and management sciences, she is an INFORMS Fellow, and she has received multiple service awards from INFORMS. She has served on the board of trustees of SIAM and on several university advisory boards. She is a member of the National Academy of Engineering. She holds more than a dozen patents, has co-authored numerous publications, and frequently speaks on analytics at conferences. She holds a BS in mathematics from UNC and an MS and PhD in operations research/information engineering from Cornell. Her personal research includes manufacturing scheduling, services resource management, transportation logistics, integer programming, and combinatorial duality. She currently leads the emerging technologies team in the IBM Watson™ group.

Dr. Emily C. Plachy is a Distinguished Engineer in Business Analytics Transformation, responsible for leading an increased use of analytics across IBM. She has integrated data analysis into her work throughout her career. Since joining IBM in 1982, she has held a number of technical leadership roles including CTO, Process, Methods, and Tools in IBM Global Business

Services® (GBS), providing architecture and technology leadership and driving the adoption of consistent methods and tools in GBS, and CTO, Enterprise Integration, GBS, providing architecture and technology leadership. She has also held a variety of roles in IBM, including development, ad tech, research, emerging business opportunities, technical sales, and services. Her technology skills include data integration, enterprise integration, solution architecture, software development, and asset reuse. She has experience in multiple industries, including banking, consumer products, retail, telecommunications, healthcare, and petroleum. She has a BS degree in applied mathematics from Washington University, an MSc degree in computer science from the University of Waterloo, and a DSc degree in computer science from Washington University. In 1992, Emily was elected to the IBM Academy of Technology, a body of approximately 1,000 of IBM's top technical leaders, and she served as its President from 2009 to 2011. She has been a long-term champion of women in technology. She is a member of Women in Technology International, the Society of Women Engineers, and INFORMS. Emily lives in New York with her husband, Tony. She is on Twitter @eplachy and on LinkedIn at http://www.linkedin.com/pub/emily-plachy/3/1bb/777.

Maureen Fitzgerald Norton, MBA, JD, is a Distinguished Market Intelligence Professional and Executive Program Manager in Business Analytics Transformation, responsible for driving the widespread use of analytics across IBM. She pioneered the development of an outcome-focused communications strategy to drive the culture change needed for analytics adoption. Maureen created analytics case studies and innovative learning exercises for teaching analytics. She co-created an innovative analytics workshop and taught MBA students in Europe and the Middle East. In her previous role, Maureen led project teams applying analytics to IBM Smarter Planet® initiatives in public safety, global social services, commerce, and merchandising, specializing in cost/benefit analysis and return on investment of analytic projects. Maureen became the first woman in IBM to earn the designation of Distinguished Market Intelligence Professional for developing innovative approaches to solving business issues and knowledge gaps through analysis. She has held a number of analytic and management roles in IBM. She earned BA and MBA degrees from the University of New Haven and a JD degree from the University of Connecticut School of Law. She is a licensed attorney and did her thesis on the legal implications of artificial intelligence. She lives in Connecticut with her husband, Dr. William Norton, and three children, Erin, Colleen, and William. She is a dual citizen of the United States and Ireland. In addition to *Analytics Across the Enterprise*,

Maureen has published "The Benefits of Social Media Analytics 2013" with the IBM Academy of Technology and "Social Media Analytics: Measuring Value Across Enterprises and Industries" in the *Journal of Management Systems*. Maureen is on Twitter @mfnorton and on LinkedIn at http://www.linkedin.com/in/maureennorton/.

I

Why Big Data and Analytics?

> *"The most competitive organizations are going to make sense of what they are observing fast enough to do something about it while they are still observing it."*
>
> —Jeff Jonas, IBM Fellow and Chief Scientist,
> Context Computing, IBM Corporation

This is the story of how an iconic company founded more than a century ago, and once deemed a "dinosaur" that would not be able to survive the 1990s, has learned lesson after lesson about survival and transformation. The use of analytics to bring more science into the business decision process is a key underpinning of this survival and transformation. Now for the first time, the inside story of how analytics is being used across the IBM enterprise is being told. According to Ginni Rometty, Chairman, President, and Chief Executive Officer, IBM Corporation, "Analytics is forming the silver thread through the future of everything we do." What is analytics? In simple terms, *analytics* is any mathematical or scientific method that augments data with the intent of providing new insight. With the nearly 1 trillion connected objects and devices generating an estimated 2.5 billion gigabytes of new data each day,[1] analytics can help discover insights in the data. That insight creates competitive advantage when used to inform actions and decisions. Data is becoming the world's new natural resource, and learning how to use that resource is a game changer.

This book will help you chart your own course to using analytics as a smarter way of driving outcomes. To get the most value from analytics, start with the strategy you are executing and apply analytics to your most important business problems. If you have thought of analytics as only a technology, this book will change that. Analytics is not just a technology; it is a *way of doing business*. Through the use of analytics, insights from data can be created to augment the gut feelings and intuition that many decisions are based on today. Analytics does not replace human judgment or diminish the creative, innovative spirit but rather informs it with new insights to be weighed in the decision process. Michael Lewis, in his book *Moneyball: The Art of Winning an Unfair Game*, describes how even in baseball, which is rooted in statistics, analytics enabled the Oakland Athletics to assemble a competitive baseball team, despite paying the third-lowest salaries.[2] Analytics for the sake of analytics will not get you far. To drive the most value, analytics should be applied to solving your most important business challenges and deployed widely. Analytics is a means, not an end. It is a way of thinking that leads to fact-based decision making.

"We believe that analytics is no longer an emerging field; today's businesses will thrive only if they master the application of analytics to all forms of data. Whether your office is a scientific lab, a manufacturing company, an emergency room, a government agency, or a professional sports stadium, there is no industry left where an analytics-trained professional cannot make a positive impact," says Brenda Dietrich, IBM Fellow and Vice President, Emerging Technologies, IBM Watson.

The intent of this book is to take some of the mystery out of how an organization can leverage big data and analytics to achieve its goals by giving current and future leaders a front-row seat to see how analytics was leveraged to transform IBM. Many consultants, academicians, and others have written eloquently on the topic of analytics, but the stories from within IBM as told by the people who learned lesson after lesson will give a real-world perspective on what works, what doesn't work, and how you can either start or accelerate your own transformation journey.

Why IBM Started an Enterprise-Wide Journey to Use Analytics

IBM has been using what we now call analytics in manufacturing and product design since the late 1950s and in supply chain operations since the 1980s. A pivotal meeting took place in 2004 between Brenda Dietrich and Linda Sanford, then Vice President of Enterprise Transformation, IBM Corporation, when IBM expanded its use of analytics from physical applications, such as supply chain and manufacturing, to applications, such as sales and finance, that did not have processes with such obvious physical characteristics, and IBM's *enterprise-wide* transformation journey to use analytics was launched.

In 2004, Dietrich led the Mathematical Sciences Department in IBM Research, a group that included a range of computational mathematics disciplines, including statistics, data mining, and operations research. Coincidentally, both Dietrich and Sanford received degrees in operations research, which is the practical application of math to real-world problems and was a precursor to much of what is now called business analytics. Sanford had seen the value of the mathematical methods developed in the Mathematical Sciences Department applied to IBM's supply chain operations.

Sanford's transformation team was looking for opportunities to build more analytics capability into IBM's overall transformation. She knew they had to put measurable successes on the board early to create a sense of credibility for their work. Dietrich and Sanford discussed the IBM sales process and the simple, easily tracked metric annual revenue per IBM seller. The goal was to increase the numerator, to generate top-line growth for the company. They started with a small pilot program, working with sales representatives in the general business group in Canada. That initial pilot was able to use IBM internal data, along with publicly available data, to score sales opportunities. The immediate results were a higher-yield pipeline for the sellers and improved revenue per seller. More importantly, they proved the power of analytics to support growth and transformation.

IBM has been an avid consumer of analytic capabilities for the past decade. Use of analytics has spread from engineering-based processes, such as product design, through logistics processes, such as supply chain operations, to human-centric processes, such as sales and workforce management. Seeing the cultural shift in the receptiveness to the use of analytics has been amazing to see. When IBM started developing sales analytics tools, many sales leaders were skeptical about the value of such tools, believing that converting an opportunity into a sale was largely a function of the seller's actions and could not be predicted in advance. But over the past decade, there has been a sea change in attitude. Now sales managers are asking for more analytics support so they can take their organizations to the next level of performance.

Big Data and Analytics Demystified

If analytics is any mathematical or scientific method that augments data with the intent of providing new insight, aren't all data queries analytics? No. Analytics is often thought of as answering questions using data, but it involves more than simple data (or database) queries. Analytics involves the use of mathematical or scientific methods to generate insight from the data.

Analytics should be thought of as a progression of capabilities, starting with the well-known methods of business intelligence, and extending through more complex methods involving significant amounts of both mathematical modeling and computation. Reporting is the most widely used analytic capability. Reporting gathers data from multiple sources, such as business automation, and creates standard summarizations of the data. Visualizations are created to bring the data to life and make it easy to interpret. As a generic example, consider store sales data from a retail chain. The data is generated through the point of sale system by reading the product bar codes at checkout. Daily reports might include total store revenue for each store, revenue by department for each region, and national revenue for each stock-keeping unit (SKU). Weekly reports might include the same metrics, as well as comparisons to the previous week and comparisons to the same week in the previous calendar year. Many reporting systems also allow for expanding the summarized data into its component parts. This is particularly useful in understanding changes in the sums. For example, a regional store manager might want to examine the store-level detail that resulted in an increase in revenue from the home entertainment department. She would be interested in knowing whether sales increased at most of the stores in the region, or whether the increase in total sales resulted from a significant sales jump in just a few stores. She might also look at whether the increase could be traced back to just a few SKUs, such as an unusually popular movie or video game. If a likely cause of the sales increase can be identified, she might alert the store managers to monitor inventory of the popular products, reposition the products within a store, or even reallocate inventory of the products across stores in her region.

Descriptive and Predictive Analytics

Reporting, also known as *descriptive analytics*, is focused on reporting what has happened, analyzing contributing data to determine why it happened, and monitoring new data to determine what is happening now. Business intelligence (BI) software provides capabilities for descriptive analytics. BI helps enterprises understand how their organization is operating by giving them a clear picture of the recent past. The deployment of BI software also requires an enterprise to carefully think about its key performance metrics, to understand what it wants to measure and monitor, and to develop some process for exploring potential causes underlying changes in measurements. Sometimes it is obvious what should be measured. Other times it is less obvious, such as when someone discovers a leading indicator of revenue through analysis. Once these capabilities have been mastered, many organizations seek to look forward and get "headlights" on what will happen in the future. They turn to *predictive analytics*, which uses techniques such as statistics and data mining to analyze current and historical information to make predictions about what will happen in the future. Predictive analytics typically produces both a prediction of what will happen and a probability that the prediction will happen.[3]

In many ways, the difference between descriptive analytics and predictive analytics is like the difference between a weather report and a weather forecast. Whereas a report describes what has happened, a forecast tells what is likely to happen and how likely it is to happen. An accurate prediction has greater business value, which is why considerable effort is applied to finding data that contains valuable signals about the future and developing analysis methods that can extract the signal effectively. In the past, performing predictive analytics had a reputation of requiring deep analytic skill. Today, modern tools have broadened the population of users who can leverage predictive analytics to augment decision making. No introduction to predictive analytics is complete without the caution that a prediction can be no better than the data that is used to make it. Thus incorrect data will likely lead to incorrect predictions, and events that have never been observed and captured in the data will never be predicted from analysis of that data.

Predicting what will happen based on the past can be quite useful. It can, for example, help a regional retail manager understand demand for a frozen dessert in the stores he manages as a function of the weather and the local competition. But, more importantly, it can also show him the relationship between past sales of this dessert and promotional pricing, coupons, and advertising. If he assumes that the same relationships will hold going forward, he can then estimate (or predict) future sales that will occur under different pricing and advertising schedules. Predictive analytics that finds relationships between actions and outcomes is particularly useful.

Prescriptive Analytics

We use the term *prescriptive analytics* to cover analytics methods that recommend actions. In general, the goal is to find a set of actions that is predicted to produce the best possible outcome. To do this, you need to understand the relationship between actions and outcomes. In many cases, that relationship is clear and (more importantly) constant. If producing and distributing a newspaper circular costs 30 cents per copy, then the cost of distributing it to any specified number of customers is clear: 30 cents multiplied by the number of customers. However, the value, in terms of increased revenue, of the circular can only be inferred by looking at past data and, for example, comparing sales in weeks during which no circular was distributed to sales in weeks in which a circular was distributed. But the inferred relationship may be different in different towns, and it may vary by week of the year. That is, the computed value must be recalculated whenever new data becomes available. Despite the limitations, it seems clear that value can be derived through careful and appropriate use of predicted relationships to make decisions. Mathematical optimization has been used for decades to recommend decisions based on known, constant relationships between actions and outcomes. It is used extensively in supply chain and logistics decisions involving scheduling and allocation of resources. More recently, it has been used for decisions where some relationships are predicted from historical data rather than being based on physical limits (for example, transportation time) or business rules (for example, economic order quantities). Examples include setting prices based on predicted price elasticity, advertising based on predicted views of the ad and predicted sales lift per viewer, and targeted promotional offers (for example, coupons at checkout) based on customer segmentation.

Social Media Analytics

Analytics can also be applied to data that does not come from within an enterprise and to data that is not easily interpreted as transactions, such as data from Twitter. Several emerging areas within analytics are already providing business value. One area is *social media analytics*, which analyzes, or "listens," to social media data to assess public opinion, or sentiment, on a variety of topics.[4] Examples of social media include blogs, micro-blogs (such as Twitter), social networking (such as Facebook), and forums. It is possible to mine social media for comments on a particular subject and analyze them for positive and negative sentiment, how people feel about a topic, or the "pulse" of a community related to a topic. A common way to communicate sentiment is to use a dashboard with views for volume trends over time, sentiment trends over time, and geographic distribution of sentiment. A frequent use of social media is to mine customer data to get feedback on products.[5] Measuring the return on investment (ROI) of using analytics for social media can present a challenge. Value driver trees (that is, visualizations of the hierarchy of influences of different value drivers) have been used to measure the value of using social media analytics for a sports clothing manufacturer, a city government, and an automotive manufacturer, among other industries.[6]

Entity Analytics

Another emerging area is *entity analytics*, which focuses on sorting through data and grouping together data that relates to the same entity. As a simple example of the power of entity analytics, consider three customer records, two of which have no data in common, and a third that has a driver's license number which is the same as that of customer record one as well as a credit card number which is the same as customer record two. These three records can be combined into one record that has more complete data than each of the three individual records. Entity analytics is a powerful technique for recognizing context and detecting like and related entities across large collections of data. Jeff Jonas, IBM Fellow and Chief Scientist, Context Computing, contends that the data enterprises have to deal with is growing so fast that enterprises are developing amnesia; that is, using the same techniques to cleanse and analyze data causes them to get behind because the amount of data is increasing so fast.[7] Jonas uses a puzzle as a metaphor for organizations' need to sort through data to make sense of it and develop context; he says that an ever-growing pile of puzzle pieces represents the ever-growing amount of data, and until you try to assemble the pieces of the puzzle or data, you do not know what you are dealing with.[8] When teaching MBA students about big data and analytics, Maureen Norton and Emily Plachy include an exercise where the students work enthusiastically to put together hundreds of puzzle pieces using multiple tables, shouting out insights as they discover them.

Cognitive Computing

Although entity analytics is helpful in finding relationships between pieces of data and can incorporate new data to either confirm or negate previously found relationships, additional methods can be applied to garner insight from unstructured data. *Cognitive computing*, computing systems that interact with people in new ways to provide insight and advice, is emerging just when we need it to help us uncover insight from the explosion of big data. Chapter 11, "Reflections and a Look to the Future," describes this exciting new era of computing.

Big Data

The most easily available source of data for analytics is an enterprise's own internal transaction data. For our retail example, this includes inventory data, sales data, employee data, and promotion and advertising data. Increasingly, enterprises are augmenting their internal data with data from external sources, including social media data. Whereas enterprise transaction data tells the retailer what has been bought, social media data can give the retailer early insight into what customers intend to buy. With the adoption of social media tools such as Twitter and the growth of blogs and forums on the Internet, the amount of social media data is growing very large, and analyzing it is providing significant insights and benefits to businesses.

Big data has four dimensions, known as the four Vs:[9]

- **Volume:** The size of data, which can range from terabytes to petabytes of data
- **Variety:** The forms of data—structured, text, multimedia
- **Velocity:** The speed at which data is available and analysis of streaming data
- **Veracity:** Data quality—managing the reliability of data

Consumers who are active in the big data social media world are driving enterprises to create collaborative systems, known as *systems of engagement*.[10] These new systems have led to the creation of engagement analytics to measure the value of engagement.[11] Engagement analytics can be used to measure employee engagement and customer engagement. Systems of engagement and engagement analytics are covered in more detail in Chapter 5, "Enabling Analytics Through Information Technology."

This book shows how IBM has solved a wide variety of business problems by leveraging analytics to elevate business results. The types of analytics described include predictive analytics, prescriptive analytics, social media analytics, and entity analytics. Some of the analytics is performed on big data. The use of analytics not only drives cost savings and revenue growth but also provides more accurate and timely information to improve decision making and reduce complexity, which helps better manage the business. Analytics gives you the ability to anticipate, and that's very powerful. So what does this mean for you? Whether you are in business for yourself or within a large company or a nonprofit or a government entity or a classroom preparing for your future, knowledge of the possibilities that analytics opens up will give you a competitive advantage. Understanding the journey that IBM has taken will shine a light on where you can get value from big data and analytics and illuminate your path to success in business.

Why Analytics Matters

"People respond to facts. Rational people will make rational decisions if you present them with the right data."

—Linda Sanford, Senior Vice President, Enterprise Transformation, IBM Corporation

Quite simply, analytics matters because it works. You can be overwhelmed with data and the value of it may be unattainable until you apply analytics to create the insights. Human brains were not built to process the amounts of data that are today being generated through social media, sensors, and more. While gut instinct is often the basis for decisions, *analytically informed intuition* is what wins going forward.

Several studies have highlighted the value of analytics. Companies that use predictive analytics are outperforming those that do not by a factor of five.[12] In a 2012 joint survey by the IBM Institute of Business Value and the Said Business School at the University of Oxford of more than 1,000 professionals around the world, 63% of respondents reported that the use of information (including big data and analytics) is creating a competitive advantage for their organizations.[13] IBM depends on analytics to meet its business objectives and provide shareholder value. The bottom line is that analytics helps the bottom line. Your competition will not be waiting to take advantage of the new insights from big data. Should you?

IBM has approached the use of analytics with a spirit of innovation and a belief that analytics will illuminate insights in data that can help improve outcomes. The company hasn't been afraid to make mistakes or redesign programs that haven't worked as planned. Unlike traditional IT projects, most analytics projects are exploratory. For example, the Development Expense Baseline Project explored innovative ways to determine development expense at a detailed level, thereby addressing a problem that many thought was impossible to solve. IBM analytic teams haven't waited for perfect data to get started; rather, they have refined and improved their data along the way. For example, the Coverage Optimization with Profitability project team described in Chapter 9, "Increasing Sales Performance," knew it had incomplete data, but rather than wait for the various data stewards to improve their data, the team jumped in and made progress incrementally on data governance and data cleansing. Using this approach will reduce your time to value. Using this approach will reduce your time to value. The key is to put a stake in the ground with a commitment that analytics will be woven into your strategy. That's how IBM does it. This approach is also effective with big data. Rather than postpone the leveraging of big data, you should embrace it, establish a link between your business priorities and your information agenda, and apply analytics to become a smarter enterprise.

Governance

A majority of clients who have engaged with IBM to learn about the internal transformation efforts are most interested in the governance topic. How do you organize to take advantage of analytics? Where do you put the analytics group? Is it an IT function? Who leads analytics projects, and who is on the team? How do you set up your organization to be able to adapt processes to incorporate analytics? Interestingly, it is organizational obstacles—not data or financial concerns—that are roadblocks to adoption of big data and analytics; examples include not knowing how to use analytics to improve the performance of the enterprise and lack of bandwidth because of competing priorities.[14]

IBM's approach has been very pragmatic and initially was quite focused in areas of the business that had the most challenges. Analytics was used as a means to address the most significant challenges first. There was a general notion that analytics could add value within IBM, but where it got very specific very fast was with large, critical problems in supply chain operations. At one point, supply chain problems were costing IBM millions of dollars per year. That story changed dramatically when using analytics become a way of doing business, and today IBM's supply chain is world class.

IBM's transformation to use analytics is part of a larger enterprise transformation that began in 1993 to transform its business processes. As part of this enterprise transformation, IBM's organization evolved to incorporate *Value Services,* defined as a group of functional units, processes, and initiatives dedicated to working collaboratively to improve productivity and effectiveness through business transformation:[15]

1. *Globally Integrated Enterprise Shared Services:* To support this transformation, globally integrated organizational units providing support services to all of IBM were formed.[16] Four of the functional areas described in the upcoming chapters are Globally Integrated Enterprise Shared Services: human resources, integrated supply chain finance, information technology, and marketing.
2. *Enterprise Transformation Initiatives:* A number of enterprise-wide initiatives were launched to drive radical, innovative transformation in the way IBM works with clients, business partners, and its own employees. Three Enterprise Transformation Initiatives, which are described in later chapters, are Development, Smarter Commerce™ Inside IBM, and Hardware Product Management Transformation.

Since they provide support services to all of IBM or drive radical, innovative transformation, Globally Integrated Enterprise Shared Services and Enterprise Transformation Initiatives are control points for leveraging analytics. For example, when Finance creates and deploys an analytic solution to predict spending, all of IBM's business units reap the benefits.

The next evolution of IBM's transformation is to migrate from a globally integrated enterprise to a smarter enterprise by optimizing the entire enterprise with the following technologies:[17]

- **Analytics** to gain business insight for customers and the enterprise
- **Social media** for business collaboration both inside and outside the enterprise
- **Mobile communications** for pervasive connectivity
- **Cloud technologies** for IT enablement

IBM's transformation to a smarter enterprise is described in "Creating a Smarter Enterprise: The Science of Transformation."[18] IBM's transformation to use analytics enterprise-wide, which began in 2004, continues; today, analytics is complemented with social, mobile, and cloud.

Many people are surprised to learn that at IBM, analytics was *not* centralized and *not* driven out of IT. Analytics is mostly thought of as a technology, and many expect technology projects to be owned by IT, but because analytics is a way of doing business, it needed to be close to the business, woven like a silver thread into the fabric of all of the business processes. The focus was on how to become smarter and more agile with the use of analytics to solve business problems; being close to those problems was required. Business analysts partner with analytics practitioners and in some cases used what IBM refers to as the "secret sauce" for analytics—IBM Research, which is a unique and differentiating function. Few companies have a 400-person math department to draw on. What does this mean for other companies? IBM has leveraged its math department both to apply analytics internally and to add some of the learnings and benefits to its analytics products and solutions. So you can get the benefit of a large math department without having to have your own.

Proven Approaches

Staying focused on solving business problems was the pragmatic start, and the other crucial element was having very high-level executive support from the beginning. From a governance perspective, those are two key levers to drive value: focus on actions and decisions that will generate value and have high-level executive sponsorship.

The ideal team to do analytics is a collaboration between an experienced data scientist,[19] a person steeped in the area of the business where the challenge needs to be solved, and an IT person with expertise in the data in that particular area of the business.

A joint study by MIT Sloan and the IBM Institute for Business Value developed several recommendations.[20] The first is that you start with your biggest and highest-value business challenge. The next recommendation is to ask a lot of questions about that challenge in order to understand what's going on or what could be going on. Then you go out and look for what data you might have that's relevant to that challenge. Finally, you determine which analytic technique can be used to analyze the data and solve the problem.

Because most companies have constraints on the amount of money and skills available for projects, estimating the ROI can provide a better differentiator for selecting the project with the highest potential impact than relying on instincts. Estimating an analytics project's ROI involves both capturing the project costs and measuring the value. As mentioned earlier in this chapter, value driver trees are an effective technique for measuring value.[21]

Analytics changes the way you approach your business and becomes an integral part of the way you manage and transform your business.

Gauging Progress

Once you've started solving business problems using big data and analytics, how do you know if your capabilities are progressing? IBM developed the Analytics Quotient (AQ) so that organizations can measure their maturity in adopting big data and analytics and set goals for enhanced adoption.[22] Based on answers to approximately 15 questions, organizations can find out if they are novices, builders, leaders, or masters.

In 2013, the IBM Institute of Business Value published results from a study focused on how to convert insights from big data and analytics into results.[23] More than 900 business and IT executives were surveyed, and through research, nine levers were identified that distinguish leaders who are able to realize value from big data and analytics from those who are not. As described in the report, the nine levers are:[24]

- **Source of Value:** Decisions that generate value
- **Measurement:** Business outcome measurement
- **Platform:** Integrated hardware and software capabilities
- **Culture:** The availability and use of data and analytics within an organization
- **Data:** Formal processes for data governance and security
- **Trust:** Confidence within the organization
- **Sponsorship:** Support and involvement of executives
- **Funding:** A rigorous analytics funding process
- **Expertise:** Development of and access to data and analytics skills

The authors found a strong link between organizations that excel in these nine levers and organizations that are deriving the greatest value from data and analytics. Further, they found that the levers do not impact the creation of value in the same way, and they identified a progression of three steps—*Enable*, *Drive*, and *Amplify*—each with three of the levers (see Figure 1-1):[25]

- *Enable* forms the foundation for creating value from big data and analytics. The foundation is actions and decisions that generate value, measuring outcomes and providing a platform for big data and analytics activities.

- *Drive* has the actions needed to create value by moving from analytics discovery to value creation, which is aided by having an analytics and big data culture, having data governance and data security, and creating trust.

- *Amplify* increases the amount of value realized by providing momentum to translate insights into actions that increase an organization's bottom line. This is done through sharing a common vision, managing and monitoring analytic investments, and knowledge-sharing opportunities.

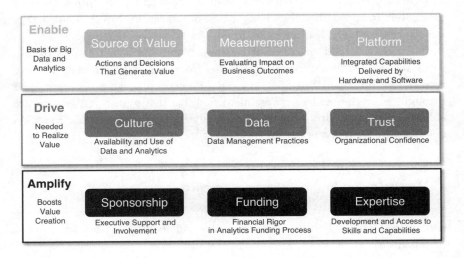

Source: "Analytics: A blueprint for value—Converting big data and analytics into results," IBM Institute for Business Value. © 2013 IBM Corporation

Figure 1-1 Nine levers: Capabilities that enable and enhance big data and analytics development, delivery, and value creation

As you start your journey to leverage big data and analytics for business value, start by leveraging the three levers in *Enable*—*Source of Value*, *Measurement*, and *Platform*—and then move to *Drive* and then finally to *Amplify*.

Overview of Nine Journeys

IBM has many business functions. Some of them are generic functions—including human resources, finance, supply chain, sales, information technology, marketing, and services—that can be found in most enterprises.

Other functions—such as software development and hardware manufacturing—are more specific to a technology company, although analogous functions exist in other industries (for example, manufacturing cars in the automotive industry).

This book contains 31 case studies of how nine business functions have incorporated analytics to change the way they do business and to improve their business results. Each business unit's story is told as a separate chapter, beginning with an overview of the unit's journey to improve its business results by levering analytics, including the pitfalls and lessons learned, followed by a more detailed description of one or more significant analytics projects within that business unit. The nine business functions started their analytics journey at different times, and they're now at different stages; they also used different approaches. Each journey is different, though we do see some common themes.

Some business units have been on long journeys, others are just starting their journeys, and others are in between. All of the business units have a history of using descriptive analytics or business intelligence. This book concentrates on predictive and prescriptive analytics and newer forms of analytics, such as social media analytics and entity analytics.

IBM's supply chain organization started its journey the earliest and has numerous analytics solutions. You will learn how the supply chain organization is using analytics to reduce expenses and to predict quality problems before there is an impact. The supply chain organization is also using social media analytics to predict supply disruptions based on events around the world. The finance organization also has a rich history of using analytics. Examples include using analytics to reduce financial risk and to reduce the risk of an acquisition failing to meet objectives. IBM's human resources (HR) organization started using analytics more recently and is using predictive analytics to proactively address retention and is using social analytics, big data, and sentiment analysis to take the "pulse" of what employees are thinking about various issues, such as a new HR program. IBM's information technology (IT) organization has developed a number of applications that leverage analytics and big data, such as how to find an employee and how to answer questions about products and services from the sales force.

Emerging Themes

You will notice some common themes in the nine IBM journeys described in this book.

Relationships inferred from data today may not be present in data collected tomorrow. The relationships that you infer from data about the past do not necessarily hold in data that you collect tomorrow. You cannot analyze data once and then make decisions forever based on old analysis. It's important to continually analyze data to verify that previously detected relationships are still valid and to discover new ones. Fortunately, major discontinuities with data do not happen very often, so change generally happens gradually. Social media sentiment, however, has a much shorter half-life than most data. Using relationships derived from past data has been repeatedly demonstrated to work better than assuming that no relationships exist. The relationships that have been detected are likely correlation rather than causality. However, these relationships, if detected and acted upon quickly, may provide at least a temporary business advantage.

You don't have to understand analytics technology to derive value from it. For a long time, many business leaders expressed the opinion that mathematics should be used by only those who understood the details of the computations. However, in recent years this view has been changing, and analytics is being treated like other technologies. You must learn how to use it effectively, but it is not necessary to understand the inner workings in order to apply analytics to business decisions. You have to apply analytics methods in the context of the problem that is being solved and make the results accessible to the end user. But just as the user of a car navigation system does not need to understand the details of the routing algorithm, the end user of analytics does not have to understand the details of the math. Typically, making the results accessible to the end user involves wrapping the math in the language and the process of the end user. Also, the analytics can be embedded deep inside things so that the user does not see it, like in supply chain operations. Analytics should be usable by anyone, not just those with PhDs in statistics or operations research. Some users will want to understand the algorithms and inner workings of an analytics model in order to trust the results prior to adoption, but they are the exception. Chapter 4, "Anticipating the Financial Future," illustrates such a case.

Fast, cheap processors and cheap storage make analysis on big data possible. Moore's law has resulted in vast increases in computing power and vast decreases in the cost of storing and accessing data. With readily available and inexpensive computing, we can do what-if calculations often and test a number of variables in big data for correlation.

Doing things fast is almost always better than doing things perfectly. Often inexact but fast approaches produce enormous gains because they result in better choices than humans would have made without the use of analytics. Over time, the approximate analytics methods can be refined and improved to achieve additional gains. However, for many business processes, there is eventually a point of diminishing returns: The calculations may become more detailed and precise, but the end results are no more accurate or valuable.

Using analytics leads to better auditability and accountability. With the use of analytics, the decision-making process becomes more structured and repeatable, and a decision becomes less dependent on the individual making the decision. When you change which people are in various positions, things still happen in the same way. You can often go back and find out what analysis was used and why a decision was made.

How to Use This Book

We have organized this book so you can choose your best path for navigating the content. The next nine chapters describe how IBM has applied analytics to address challenges in nine different business functions. Some may choose to read the chapters sequentially. Others can instead start with the chapters that are of the most interest to them.

This book can also be used as a reference. The appendix includes a table of the 31 case studies described in this book, including the challenges and outcomes, along with the type of data and analytics techniques used to achieve the outcomes. Using the table, you can map from a particular analytics technique to a business challenge and then map to a chapter and page that describes the challenge. For example, if social media analytics is of interest, the table shows that Chapter 2, "Creating a Smarter Workforce," describes how IBM's HR organization uses social media analytics to gain an accurate view of what employees are thinking and that Chapter 3, "Optimizing the Supply Chain," describes how the supply chain organization uses social media analytics to predict disruptions in the supply chain. You can also examine the table to see if the business challenge you are facing is similar to one in the table.

Analytics Across the Enterprise can be used as a text for or a complement to the textbooks for MBA or undergraduate classes with analytics content as it provides real-world examples of using analytics to transform business areas and improve results. We chose nine as the number of business area stories to include so that these nine chapters, along with this chapter and Chapter 11 would fit into a semester-long course.

This book describes how nine different organizations are using analytics as a way of doing business and how they are realizing business value from data and analytics. Throughout this book, you will learn about the business problems selected, the pitfalls encountered, the business value that can be obtained by using big data and analytics, and the many lessons the teams learned along the way.

Endnotes

1. 2013 IBM Annual Report, IBM Corporation, page 13. http://www.ibm. com/annualreport/2013/.
2. Lewis, M., *Moneyball: The Art of Winning an Unfair Game*, W. W. Norton & Company, 2004.
3. Siegel, E., *Predictive Analytics: The Power to Predict Who Will Click, Buy, Lie, or Die*, Wiley, 2013.
4. Leskovec, J., "Tutorial: Analytics & Predictive Models for Social Media," Stanford University, 2011. http://snap.stanford.edu/proj/socmedia-www/.
5. Elsas, J. L., and Glance, N., "Shopping for Top Forums: Discovering Online Discussion for Product Research," *Proceedings of the First Workshop on Social Media Analytics*, ACM, New York, 2010. http://dl.acm.org/citation.cfm?id=1964862&CFID=389807816&CFTOKEN=33144969.
6. Kadochnikov, N., and Norton, M., "Social Media Analytics: Measuring Value Across Enterprises and Industries," *Journal of Management Systems*, Volume 23, Number 1, 2013.
7. Jonas, J., "Enterprise Amnesia Versus Enterprise Intelligence," IBM Redbooks Video, TIPS0924, 2013. http://www.redbooks.ibm.com/abstracts/tips0924.html?Open.
8. Ibid.
9. Schroeck, M., et al., "Analytics: The Real-World Use of Big Data—How Innovative Enterprises Extract Value from Uncertain Data," IBM Institute for Business Value, 2012. http://www-03.ibm.com/systems/hu/resources/the_real_word_use_of_big_data.pdf.
10. Moore, G., "Systems of Engagement and the Future of Enterprise IT—A Sea Change in Enterprise IT," AIIM, 2011. http://www.google.com/url?sa=t&rct=j&q=&esrc=s&source=web&cd=1&cad=rja&ved=0CDQ QFjAA&url=http%3A%2F%2Fwww.aiim.org%2F~%2Fmedia%2F Files%2FAIIM%2520White%2520Papers%2FSystems-of-Engagement.pdf&ei=sPL0Uu6zGcXY0gGFzoCYDQ&usg= AFQjCNFSo9Ne5zPwcdPEYQsaceW6g5JnBg&sig2=bI-sNdgSnumdHzstwxh6PA&bvm=bv.60799247,d.cWc.

11. Wallace, M., "Maximize the Value of Your Systems of Engagement," IBM Corporation. http://www.ibm.com/engage.

12. LaValle, S., et al., "Analytics: The New Path to Value—How the Smartest Organizations Are Embedding Analytics to Transform Insights into Action," IBM Institute for Business Value, 2010. http://public.dhe.ibm.com/common/ssi/ecm/en/gbe03371usen/GBE03 371USEN.PDF.

13. Schroeck, M., et al., "Analytics: The Real-World Use of Big Data."

14. LaValle, S., et al., "Analytics: The New Path to Value."

15. Urso, D. L., et al., "Enterprise Transformation: The IBM Journey to Value Services," *IBM Journal of Research and Development*, Volume 56, Number 6, November/December 2012. http://ieeexplore.ieee.org/ xpl/articleDetails.jsp?tp=&arnumber=6353958&queryText%3 Denterprise+transformation+IBM+journey.

16. DeViney, N., et al., "Becoming a Globally Integrated Enterprise: Lessons on Enabling Organization and Cultural Change," *IBM Journal of Research and Development*, Volume 56, Number 6, November/December 2012. http://ieeexplore.ieee.org/xpl/articleDetails.jsp?tp= &arnumber=6353944&queryText%3Dbecoming+a+globally+ integrated.

17. Butner, K., "Creating a Smarter Enterprise: The Science of Transformation," IBM Institute for Business Value, 2013. http://public.dhe. ibm.com/common/ssi/ecm/en/gbe03584usen/GBE03584USEN.PDF.

18. Ibid.

19. Rao, A., "The 5 Dimensions of the So-Called Data Scientist," Emerging Technology Blog, Pricewaterhouse Coopers, March 5, 2014. http:// usblogs.pwc.com/emerging-technology/the-5-dimensions-of-the-so-called-data-scientist/.

20. LaValle, S., et al., "Analytics: The New Path to Value."

21. Kadochnikov, N., and Norton, M., "Social Media Analytics: Measuring Value Across Enterprises and Industries."

22. "From Novice to Master: Understanding the Analytics Quotient Maturity Model," IBM Canada, Ltd., 2011. http://public.dhe.ibm.com/ common/ssi/ecm/en/ytw03169usen/YTW03169USEN.PDF.

23. Balboni, F., et al., "Analytics: A Blueprint for Value—Converting Big Data and Analytics Insights into Results," IBM Institute for Business Value, 2013. http://public.dhe.ibm.com/common/ssi/ecm/en/ gbe03575usen/GBE03575USEN.PDF.

24 Ibid., page 5.

25. Ibid., page 6.

2

Creating a Smarter Workforce

"Big data and analytics is the entry point for human resources to inte-grate with operations because it has empirical evidence, not just instincts."

—Randy MacDonald, former Senior Vice President, Human Resources, IBM Corporation

Perspective: Applying Analytics to the Workforce

Human capital is the leading cited source of sustained economic value in a global study of CEOs.[1] Using analytics to optimize the recruitment and management of employees can provide significant business results. In fact, new terms, such as *workforce analytics*, *talent analytics*,[2] and others have been coined to capture the use of analytics to optimize and make better decisions about people in the workforce. Gartner defines *workforce analytics* as "an advanced set of data analysis tools and metrics for comprehensive workforce performance measurement and improvement."[3] Workforce analytics thus encompasses analysis of all the aspects of the workforce life cycle: hiring, training and development, retention, assignment, and compensation and benefits. Using analytics to optimize the management and cost of employees can lead to improvements in an organization's profitability. Even more valuable are the opportunities that analytics can provide to organizational performance. For example, engagement analytics applied to a system of engagement can be used to increase employee engagement,[4] which can lead to better organizational performance and cultural change. Analytics can also be used to predict which employees have a propensity to leave so that actions can be taken to help retain critical employees.

More than 10 years ago, IBM realized that the workforce represented a significant opportunity for the application of analytics. It began to capture information about employees' skills and roles and to understand processes used to determine near- and long-term employee skills requirements. As in supply chains of physical goods, many of the analytics opportunities in workforce management require resolving demand—represented by job roles, tasks, projects, or other units of work—with supply—represented by skills, experience, individual employees, teams, or other units of capacity to do work. When long-term shortages in supply are predicted, there are opportunities to optimize recruitment, retention, and training. IBM has created tools to help its employees characterize their capabilities and skills, and it uses text analytics and other means of analyzing unstructured data to determine an individual's skills from a resume and other digital evidence of experience. Describing the skills required for a specific job or task is relatively straightforward, and IBM can rank individuals for jobs or tasks based on skill match by using a variety of analytics methods. Matching a group of individuals to a set of jobs or tasks, however, is slightly more challenging because it involves assigning one and only one person to each job and trading off individual (pairwise) matches for an overall assignment that fills all jobs. Fortunately, the operations research profession has been studying this problem for decades, and effective algorithms and software are readily available.[5] Chapter 10, "Delivering Services with Excellence," describes how constraint programming can be used to match people with positions and generate near-optimal assignments.

Moving beyond near-term capacity assessment and employee assignment, IBM Research began to study the use of predictive analytics in workforce management. An early project in this area involved predicting the future composition of IBM's workforce, based on historical hiring, training, promotion, and attrition rates. A later project involved predicting attrition by job type, business unit, and geography, based on historical data; this project sought to understand, again from the data, the impact of various factors, such as salary, training, promotion, and management contact, on these rates.

Murray Campbell, Senior Manager, IBM Research, and a contributor to the Smarter Workforce initiative, observed: "One of the next big trends in Smarter Workforce is that big data will help us build much more effective and more predictive models for getting the right people in an organization, getting them in the right job, figuring out what skills are best to have, both now and in the future, and what factors help people become more engaged employees." Another big trend in the workforce is the increasing use of social media, which is providing leaders and managers with even greater insights into the patterns of employee behavior, which will help in the recruitment and development of employees and in employee collaboration. For example, network analysis of employee interactions on social media can be used to assess patterns of sharing and influence, as well as identify isolated communities of people.

Other companies besides IBM have recognized the role of data and analytics in workforce management. In 2000, Kenexa®, a recruitment services and consulting company, exited its temporary staffing business to focus on screening and behavioral assessment in support of recruiting and skill-testing technologies. Rudy Karsan, CEO and Founder of Kenexa, came to the realization that much more could be done for people than merely focus on just knowledge, skills, and attributes. Over the next decade, Kenexa built a portfolio of recruitment, learning, and compensation tools and a significant repository of data based on engagement surveys and attribute testing. The Kenexa team joined IBM in 2012, bringing with it significant expertise in organizational psychology. For example, Kenexa can assess whether a potential candidate for employment is a good fit for the culture of a company and use predictive modeling to predict which interviewees are likely to stay for more than two years as well as which candidates are potential leaders. This capability, which assesses individuals in the context of specific roles and company cultures, complements the methods previously developed within IBM, which compute how many people from a large employee population are likely to stay in a job by estimating the likelihood that a specific individual will stay in his or her job.

Recently, Karsan began thinking about how big data is changing the game of analytics and decision making. In the past, to gather insight from data, you would develop a hypothesis and collect data to prove or disprove it. Now, with the decreasing cost of storage and the ease of collecting data, you do not have to start with hypotheses; you can simply analyze the data and see what it tells you.[6] For example, Kenexa used big data to learn that, in a retail operation at the entry level or at a cashier job family, the number-one driver of turnover was duration of commute. This was initially a surprise, and

Kenexa would not have thought up a hypothesis for this, until the big data provided this insight. After some thought, though, this insight made sense because many of the cashiers were single parents and did not want to spend a large part of their day at work or commuting to work. With big data, you need to look at the data without preconceived ideas and see what it says.

> *"We are reinventing work, replacing guess work with precision. Science and data will allow us to do this in a much more superior fashion than in the past."*
>
> —Rudy Karsan, CEO and Founder, Kenexa

To learn about the use of and challenges with workforce analytics, IBM surveyed more than 400 North American human resources professionals. The findings support the following themes:[7]

- Workforce analytics plays an increasingly important role in addressing strategic human capital challenges.
- Workforce analytics is a key capability for HR organizations seeking a more proactive role in driving business strategy.
- The implementation of workforce analytics continues to be hindered by both technical and skill-related issues.

Randy MacDonald, then IBM Senior Vice President, Human Resources, observed that numbers are persuasive in meetings with the CEO. In some companies, the Chief Human Resources Officer (CHRO) is one of the least quantitative of the C-level executives, and, before 2010, this was true for IBM. In 2010, to drive the use of analytics in HR, MacDonald identified one of his existing HR directors, Jonathan Ferrar, to lead the new global function of HR workforce analytics.

Having a strong stakeholder was critical to Ferrar's success. MacDonald gave Ferrar a mandate and the people he needed to embed analytics into the culture of IBM's HR organization and to increase the use of data analysis to inform and support business decisions. Ferrar started with a group of people whose previous role had involved preparing reports on various aspects of HR and who managed the HR data warehouse. One of the early challenges he faced was the lack of knowledge about analytics that existed in the HR organization. This was overcome through education and infusion of a few analytics experts, together with partnerships with parts of IBM more experienced in analytics. Ferrar's experience of transforming an existing group of employees into an analytics team is the norm in competitive markets, where it is not sensible to hire an entirely new analytics team, none of whom would have the institutional knowledge, context, or cultural awareness of the organization that are important in applying analytics.

In just a few years, Ferrar's analytics organization tackled projects and achieved positive results in predictive attrition, labor risk analysis, and understanding of social sentiment of IBM employees. Each of these projects was challenging, for different reasons: the first because of the large volume of data, the second because of the length of research time needed to validate models for predictability, and the third because of the technology required, which did not exist in easy-to-consume software at the time. When asked why he tackled these difficult analytics projects, Ferrar replied, "You have to answer the questions that are being asked by the business leaders, and if this means tackling hard problems, then that's what you must do." Ferrar uses "hard" metrics, such as measuring ROI, to gauge his success. He also developed "soft" measures to track the changes in quantitative attitude of his organization, such as noting the adoption of analytics training and how much HR employees began to use the "language of analytics" in interactions with each other and with business leaders.

Challenge: Retaining High-Value Resources in Growth Markets

Retaining high-value, skilled employees is a challenge for most businesses. A survey of more than 400 North American human resources professionals found that the ability to retain talent is ranked 89% for importance and 51% for effectiveness.[8] Competition for skills is particularly intense in growth markets, such as India and China, where the number of jobs is growing more rapidly than the number of applicants, creating an environment where people have a number of opportunities for jobs. Attrition is costly to companies, causing loss of productivity, hiring and onboarding costs, and salary premiums in countries with rapidly growing economies or when hiring skills that are in short supply. The total costs of replacing an employee who leaves can range from 90% to 200% of that employee's salary.[9] Using predictive analytics to proactively identify high-value skilled employees at risk of leaving could provide insights to proactively address the risk factors and improve retention.

IBM's services delivery workforce in GBS in India was experiencing a high rate of attrition that was impacting business and launched a proactive retention project to address the problem. IBM designed a process and developed a model that could accurately predict workers at risk of leaving and then make recommendations on actions to take to retain them. For example, some of the recommendations were to address concerns with compensation or the pace of promotions. The solution involves clustering the resource of interest by criteria such as country, business unit, and job category. Clustering refers to grouping a set of data so that data within each cluster is similar and data from different clusters is not similar. For each cluster, the voluntary attrition versus the compensation is determined along with the resulting ROI.

Outcome: Attrition Rate Declined; Net Benefits Exceeded Expectations

This project had an impact on the attrition rate, causing it to decline. The project achieved 325% of the ROI for the 2012–2013 investment.

Challenge: Gaining an Accurate View of What Employees Are Thinking

In January 2011, MacDonald recognized that social analytics is a game changer for an HR organization. His question was: Can we get better insight than that provided by surveys by using social media to get a more accurate, more comprehensive, and more immediate view of what employees are thinking? To answer this question, Ferrar launched a project to understand sentiments that were being expressed through social media. The project became known as **Enterprise Social Pulse**.

A team started a project using IBM Social Media Analytics to capture the collective voice of the enterprise. Examples of questions of interest included: What are IBM employees talking about? How do they feel about the new products, services, or programs? What do they think of the company? How do they feel about working for IBM?

Enterprise Social Pulse has several guiding principles for data usage, including collecting data from only publicly available data and anonymizing all data. An early challenge was ensuring that employees' data could not be analyzed at the level of an individual and that the aggregate data was specific enough to be useful while general enough to be representative. The IBM

Research team in Cambridge provided an elegant solution that allows analytics, segmentation, and insights to be performed on the social media data without ever revealing the authors' identities.

Enterprise Social Pulse provides much value to IBM. Employees are able to influence HR practices and offerings by expressing their opinion. IBM HR professionals now have the ability to use employee engagement surveys to assess the engagement of the organization at a specific point in time and to gather insights expressed on internal and external public social media to provide insights in "near real time." When necessary, HR professionals can follow up with targeted surveys and focus groups to gain information on identified issues.

Enterprise Social Pulse has evolved into an enterprise-oriented employee sentiment analysis solution that provides consumable strategic insights to decision makers about people-related topics based on internal and external social media data that is anonymized to respect the individuals' privacy.[10] A primary objective of Enterprise Social Pulse is to foster a social business environment within IBM. To enable this objective, HR has made available a widget that gives employees a quick snapshot of what the chatter has been, by country, over the past 30 days.

Enterprise Social Pulse listens to and ingests social media content (publicly posted data on IBM Connections and tweets from IBM employees who tweet on Twitter). Next, authors' demographic characteristics are augmented with the social media content, while the identity gets obfuscated. The text is then analyzed for sentiment to create interactive visualizations displaying the most-discussed topics and the sentiment around them, aggregated by demographic segments. To derive sentiment about a topic, Enterprise Social Pulse started with the preconfigured set of sentiment terms and concepts in IBM Social Media Analytics and added to these terms, when necessary. For example, words such as *wonderful* and *outstanding* indicate positive sentiment, and words such as *awful* and *terrible* indicate negative sentiment.

Outcome: Ability to Act on Real Insights About Employees

Figure 2-1 is a visualization of countries colored according to their sentiment value for a particular topic. Sentiment is typically displayed using colors rather than shades of gray. (To see a color version of this figure, go to http://www.ibmpressbooks.com/title/9780133833034.)

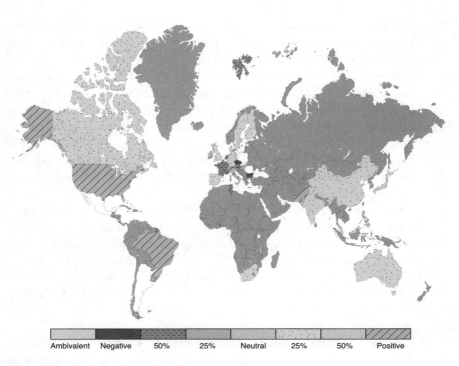

Ambivalent   Negative   50%   25%   Neutral   25%   50%   Positive

Figure 2-1   World map visualization of sentiment

Enterprise Social Pulse detects patterns in what people are talking about by analyzing the data in real time. Because of the large amount of data, the many different types of data, and real-time analysis, Enterprise Social Pulse is a big data solution, covering three of the four Vs of big data: *Volume*, *Variety*, and *Velocity* (see Chapter 1, "Why Big Data and Analytics?").[11] Issues that are being discussed the most are weighted more heavily. Enterprise Social Pulse can serve as an early warning system by bringing issues to the surface early. Figure 2-2 shows a timeline view. The bars are colored by sentiment time and sized according to daily volume, allowing an analyst to visualize how the volume of snippets varies over time. (To see a color version of this figure, go to http://www.ibmpressbooks.com/title/9780133833034.)

Enterprise Social Pulse started with English language sentiment. More languages are planned for the future. To date, data to be analyzed by Enterprise Social Pulse is "passively" collected: Collection today relies solely on employees' personal use of the social platforms. In the future, social "mini-polls" will be used to more actively gather data and complement the data currently collected from the social platforms.

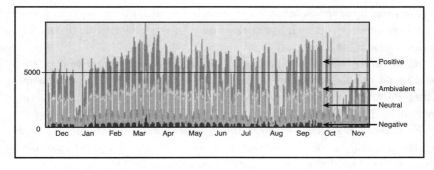

Figure 2-2   Timeline visualization of sentiment

When asked about the significance of Enterprise Social Pulse, Stela Lupushor, Workforce Analytics Leader, IBM Corporation, said, "If we have a solution that allows us to listen to the voice of the employees, make sense of all the chatter and glean insights and influence decisions that are being made in the enterprise, and if you show the employees that you care about what they say, we will create the virtuous cycle of improvement and engagement with our workforce."

Lessons Learned

Measure to gauge success. Ferrar learned very early the importance of measuring progress, both using hard measurements and soft measurements. The Proactive Retention project is a good example of measuring ROI to gauge success.

The accuracy of sentiment analysis has to be continuously refined according to human language nuances. Despite the advances in human–computer speech interaction, computers have a lot to learn from humans about the use of language. In particular, sarcasm and humor are very difficult for an algorithm to detect. The unstructured data used in social media also includes a wide variety of typographical errors as well as individual characteristics such as the use of abbreviations and emoticons. Moving from manual techniques to fix obvious errors to machine learning in sentiment analysis is highly desirable.

Participation in social media is a relatively new behavior. The lack of widespread, intense social media behavior, especially in certain demographic population segments, has slowed the pace of results in terms of measuring IBM's social pulse. Results might not always be representative of the organizational demographics.

The value is the actions taken, not the insight. As with other analytics projects that have reports and insights as their output, the major value occurs when action is taken based on insight.

Relationships inferred from data today may not be present in data collected tomorrow. Social media sentiment, in particular, has a shorter half-life than most other data. New topics can emerge suddenly, and opinion can change overnight.

Fast, cheap processors and cheap storage make analysis on big data possible. Sentiment analysis of vast amounts of social media is a good example of analysis that would not have been practical a few years ago.

You don't have to understand analytics technology to derive value from it. The Enterprise Social Pulse widget, which gives employees access to 30 days of chatter, is an example of getting the benefit of sentiment analysis without needing to know how it works.

Doing things fast is almost always better than doing things perfectly. By working incrementally, the HR department gained value early, while working to refine techniques over time. Another advantage of working incrementally is that awareness can be driven early, though this needs to be balanced with managing expectations. For proactive retention, acting on a model that is only 80% accurate is valuable because people can decide to leave suddenly. Predicting that a person will leave after they have left is not of much value. Enterprise Social Pulse is still experimental and is being continuously improved.

It's important to leverage the levers. As discussed in Chapter 1, organizations that excel in leveraging the nine levers of differentiation are deriving the most value from data and analytics.[12] IBM's HR organization has made good use of the capabilities in all nine of the levers of differentiation that enable organizations to create value from their data. At the *Enable* level, because proactive retention projects demonstrate significant business results, *Source of Value* is leveraged; HR measures the impact on business outcomes, so *Measurement* is leveraged; and analytics solutions run on several standard *Platforms*, depending on the requirements. At the *Drive* level, MacDonald and Ferrar created a *Culture* in HR for the use of data and analytics; HR *Data* has processes for governance and security; and HR has organizational confidence, demonstrating *Trust*. At the *Amplify* level, strong *Sponsorship* exits, which provides support of the application of analytics to gather insights about the workforce to aid in decision making; HR's *Funding* model for analytics projects has financial rigor; and HR has developed a team with analytics *Expertise*. The nine levers are working: HR is getting value from its data and is positioned to derive additional value in the future.

Endnotes

1. "Leading Through Connections—Insights from the Global Chief Executive Officer Study," IBM Institute of Business Value, May, 2012, page 17. http://www-935.ibm.com/services/us/en/c-suite/ceostudy2012/downloads.html.

2. Davenport, T., Harris, J. and Shapiro, J., "Competing on Talent Analytics," *Harvard Business Review*, October 2010.

3. Gartner, *IT Glossary*. http://www.gartner.com/it-glossary/?s=smarter+workforce.

4. Wallace, M., "Maximize the Value of Your Systems of Engagement," IBM Corporation. www.ibm.com/engage.

5. Burkard, R., Dell'Amico, M., and Martello, S., *Assignment Problems* (revised reprint), Society for Industrial and Applied Mathematics, 2012. http://www.assignmentproblems.com.

6. Mayer-Schonberger, V., and Cukier, K., *Big Data: A Revolution That Will Transform How We Live, Work, and Think*, Houghton Mifflin Harcourt Publishing Company, 2013.

7. "Getting Smart About Your Workforce: Why Analytics Matter," IBM Global Business Services, March, 2009. http://www-935.ibm.com/services/us/gbs/bus/pdf/getting-smart-about-your-workforce_wp_final.pdf.

8. Ibid.

9. "Differences in Employee Turnover Across Key Industries," Executive Brief, Society for Human Resource Management, December 2011. https://www.shrm.org/Research/benchmarks/Documents/Assessing%20Employee%20Turnover_FINAL.pdf.

10. Shami, N. S., et al., "Understanding Employee Social Media Chatter with Enterprise Social Pulse," *Proceedings of the ACM Conference on Computer Supported Cooperative Work Companion*, 2014. http://dl.acm.org/citation.cfm?id=2531650.

11. Schroeck, M., et al., "Analytics: The Real-World Use of Big Data—How Innovative Enterprises Extract Value from Uncertain Data," IBM Institute for Business Value, 2012. http://www-03.ibm.com/systems/hu/resources/the_real_word_use_of_big_data.pdf.

12. Balboni, F., et al., "Analytics: A Blueprint for Value—Converting Big Data and Analytics Insights into Results," IBM Institute for Business Value, 2013. http://public.dhe.ibm.com/common/ssi/ecm/en/gbe03575usen/GBE03575USEN.PDF.

3

Optimizing the Supply Chain

"If the execution guys aren't willing to embrace the tool and make it part of their process, then it's just 'fun math.'"

—Donnie Haye, Vice President, Analytics, Solutions and Acquisitions, IBM Integrated Supply Chain, IBM Corporation

Perspective: Applying Analytics to the Supply Chain

No single organization has been as central to IBM's transformation success over the past decade as the Integrated Supply Chain (ISC). A significant part of IBM's transformation was founded on the strategy of establishing common global processes to drive efficiency by eliminating redundancies and sharing best practices. The ISC led the way in driving this process integration across core operations for IBM, including procurement, manufacturing, and fulfillment from multinational towers to a globally integrated enterprise. In 2001, IBM created the ISC organization, a single business unit charged with making the company's supply chain one that increases market share, grows revenue and profit, improves cash flow, and enhances client satisfaction.

Because the supply chain was successful in delivering significant cost savings, establishing global talent leadership, and driving core process improvements, the organization's influence was expanded. The scope of responsibility of IBM's ISC is broader than that of most large enterprise supply chains. Beyond the traditional responsibilities for planning, sourcing, making, delivering, and returning,[1] the ISC is responsible for presales support and cash collection for all sales transactions. In addition, while typical supply chains deal with physical production and finished goods (hardware manufacturing, in the case of IBM), the ISC also owns "opportunity to order" for cash processes for all software, technical services, and business process services, as well as some aspects of deal financing. *Opportunity to order* is a sales process that starts when an opportunity to make a sale to a client is first identified and ends when the order is captured (or lost and is no longer tracked). Figure 3-1 shows the expansion of the ISC's role over time:

- The inner circle shows the supply chain core functions of manufacturing, supplier orders, and logistics.
- The middle circle shows responsibilities of the ISC expanded to include presales support and cash collection and functions such as business partner processes, invoice and cash collection, and contract management.
- Finally, the outer circle shows the most recent expansion of responsibilities, related to opportunity to order management, analytics, and the transformation of supply chain applications to leverage mobile and cloud technologies.

When Fran O'Sullivan was named General Manager, IBM Integrated Supply Chain, in 2010, she recognized that further horizontal integration across the supply chain with IBM business units was a major transformational opportunity.

O'Sullivan also observed a grassroots interest in analytics, with some analytics projects dating from the 1980s, and a belief in the value of analytics. However, she found a localized project funding and selection model and a number of advanced analytics projects that were not coordinated. O'Sullivan recognized that the ISC was very data rich and that by leveraging analytics, she would be able to drive optimization of the supply chain to new levels and improve business results. O'Sullivan pulled together all of the analytics projects and formed a new organization, named Smarter Supply Chain Analytics (SSCA), with Donnie Haye as its Vice President. Incorporating analytics into the ISC's transformation was a natural evolution.

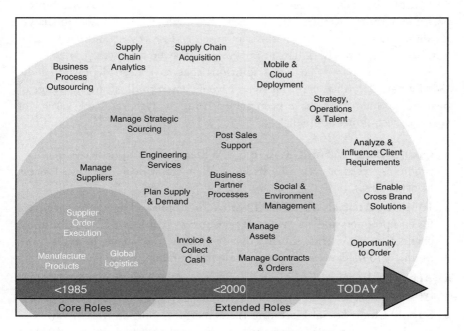

Figure 3-1 Evolution of roles of IBM's Integrated Supply Chain organization

The mission of SSCA includes analytics strategy development; analytics project design, development, and implementation; collaboration across IBM brands; and solution commercialization, client sales, and delivery support. The SSCA drives building a smarter supply chain with analytics for significant business benefit.

> *"IBM demonstrates the value of Smarter Commerce through a company with a very large supply chain—namely itself. IBM's Integrated Supply Chain (ISC) applies analytics to drive effectiveness...doing more with less. This is not only beneficial to IBM, but the lessons learned can be translated to clients with large supply chains as well."*
>
> —David Hill, Principal, Mesabi Group LLC

IBM's supply chain analytics focuses on providing insight to optimize both IBM's business processes and the client experience. SSCA has built a portfolio of more than 30 analytics assets, has deployed these assets in analytics solutions spanning the entire set of enterprise processes, and has realized hundreds of millions of dollars of improvements over a five-year horizon.

From the numerous analytics solutions that have been deployed in the ISC, four are described here. These four were chosen to illustrate the range of business problems that have been solved using analytics and the variety of analytics techniques applied:

- **Quality Early Warning System (QEWS)** detects and prioritizes quality problems weeks or even months sooner than traditional Statistical Process Control (SPC).

- **IBM Buy Analysis Tool (iBAT)** provides supply and demand visibility for end products and an analytical platform to enable better distribution channel management, ensuring that channel partners have the right products to meet client demand while minimizing inventory.

- **Accounts Receivable—Next Best Action (NBA)** uses advanced analytics to optimize resources required in the collection of revenues.

- **Supply Chain Social Listening** is an emerging solution that monitors social media channels for information that could have an effect on IBM's supply chain.

Challenge: Detecting Quality Problems Early

In 2006, at a time when IBM was having major quality issues with the memory components on its high-end server, Ross Mauri, then IBM General Manager, System P®, traveled to IBM Research to seek help. There he met Emmanuel Yashchin, a Statistician in the IBM Research Mathematical Sciences department. The challenge presented to Yashchin involved conflicting goals: come up with a data analysis procedure that detects quality problems and keeps the number of false alarms as low as possible. Yashchin discussed with Mauri how the Cumulative Sum (CUSUM) sequential analysis technique could be used to detect the memory problems while keeping the number of false positives low.[2]

Mauri approved the technique, a team was formed with people from Research and the ISC, and CUSUM was used as the basis for the **Quality Early Warning System (QEWS)**. IBM Research took responsibility for the calculation engine and documentation, and the ISC took responsibility for the data preparation and the end-user dashboard. Incorporating CUSUM into a solution for real-world quality management required overcoming several significant technical challenges:[3]

- Significant computational power was required.
- CUSUM needed to scale to an enterprise-wide implementation.
- Difficulties in interpreting data needed to be overcome.
- Quality professionals needed to understand CUSUM.

QEWS is one of the ISC's big data analytics solutions. QEWS is deployed upstream at suppliers, deployed in IBM's operations, and deployed to many products operating in the field, and it ingests attribute and parametric data from thousands and thousands of point sources from across the supply chain. Remember from Chapter 1, "Why Big Data and Analytics?" that big data can be characterized by four Vs.[4] QEWS data has two of the four big data Vs: *Volume* and *Velocity*.

The established technique for detection of quality problems is Statistical Process Control (SPC), which uses statistical methods. A drawback with conventional SPC stems from the Western Electric decision rules for detecting "out-of-control" conditions on control charts.[5] For example, one of the rules specifies that eight consecutive points falling on one side of the centerline should trigger an alarm. This trigger may not be valuable if the data involved is close to the centerline, as such types of excursions could easily turn out to be spurious or unimportant. In contrast, the CUSUM approach ignores such a condition if the excursion does not indicate anything serious. Thus, QEWS, based on CUSUM, tends to detect quality problems early while keeping the number of false alarms low.

Anticipating skepticism about yet another quality process, the team devised a way to build support for the new tool. As soon as the team had a prototype, it asked potential user groups to provide historical data associated with some previously addressed but very difficult quality issue. The team was not told when the problem occurred, what it was, or what action was taken. By inputting these data sets into QEWS, and sharing its findings with the data and process owners, the team was able to demonstrate that QEWS could indeed detect problems much earlier than could traditional SPC. This helped build support and demand for the tool throughout the ISC.

QEWS identifies quality trends well before they are detectable using traditional SPC and prioritizes problems with few false alarms. It creates alerts that enable IBM and its suppliers to proactively detect and manage quality issues at any stage in the product life cycle. It also has an effective dashboard for quick navigation of big data. The dashboard provides a customizable view of comprehensive information and allows drill-down to more detailed information. Figure 3-2 compares the times of detection of a problem using QEWS and traditional SPC. The arrow labeled QEWS Alert at the bottom of the figure indicates the point in time when QEWS detected a problem. The arrow labeled SPC Alert at the right of the figure indicates the point in time when SPC identified an alert—that is, when a point first fell outside the specified control limits. QEWS gave an alert when the cumulative evidence crossed above its horizontal threshold line, which is not shown in this figure. In this example, QEWS detected the problem six weeks earlier than SPC did. (To see a color version of this figure, go to http://www.ibmpressbooks.com/title/9780133833034.)

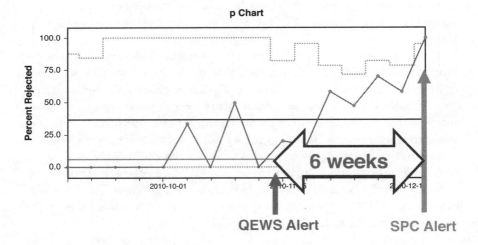

Figure 3-2 Quality alert comparison of QEWS and SPC

Outcome: Significant Cost Savings, Improved Productivity, Improved Brand Value, and Two Awards

QEWS provides significant cost savings in manufacturing by reducing rework and scrap, provides improved productivity in manufacturing and engineering by enabling higher quality, and provides improved brand value through increased customer satisfaction. Since its deployment, QEWS has contributed approximately $10 million per year in total cost reduction.

After IBM used this solution internally, it made QEWS available externally, as part of Predictive Maintenance and Quality (PMQ) 2.0. IBM has been recognized for QEWS with two awards: a Leading Innovator Award from *Information Week* in 2012[6] and the Institute for Supply Management (ISM) award for Excellence in Supply Management.

Challenge: Providing Supply/Demand Visibility and Improved Channel Inventory Management

Many of IBM's hardware products are sold through distributors and resellers. IBM relies on business partners to maintain correct inventory levels. Managing the right channel inventory, at a part-number level, is a very tough balancing act. Holding too little inventory of a part number results in stock-outs, unhappy end customers, and lost sales. Holding too much inventory results in many types of increased inventory holding costs for partners, costs of promotions to sell aged inventory for both IBM and partners, and increased price protection costs, as technology components and end products usually come down in price over time. IBM incurs these price protection costs for reimbursements made to its channel partners based on the inventory impacted by price reductions.

In 2007, IBM's Systems and Technology Group (STG) launched a business transformation initiative focused on improving inventory management in the channel to reduce costs while improving serviceability. The status quo was not optimal for IBM or its business partners. In collaboration with STG, the Business Partner organization, and the ISC, IBM Research began work on a web-based collaboration and analytics solution. The team faced multiple challenges: diverse product sets with short product life cycles, multiple channel partners serving a common customer base, and highly seasonal end-customer demand with big one-time deals masking demand trends. In response to the challenges, the IBM Research team, working with the University of Michigan, developed an industry-first inventory–cost trade-off model for price protection contracts.[7] The inventory model was complemented by an online forecasting algorithm that estimated future demand at IBM's channel partners, using available sales and technology data, order skew information, product life cycle position, and short-term order trends. These data feeds, which are from many downstream signals, have the big data dimension of *Volume*.[8] Together, the inventory model and forecasting engine were integrated into a web-based collaboration system called **IBM Buy Analysis Tool (iBAT)**, which provided up-to-date visibility and replenishment recommendations for partners to maintain recommended inventory levels. The inventory recommendations generated by the optimization model indicated the minimum inventory needed to cover future demand subject to demand uncertainty and variable supply lead times, up to IBM-recommended target service levels. All of this was provided daily, at the part number level.

Once the initial prototype was ready, the first step of the transformation journey was complete. The next step was adoption. The team worked with one of the largest distributors to test the system. The team gave the partner access to the iBAT prototype so they could log in and view the dashboard, getting access to key inventory metrics, demand trends, and iBAT replenishment buy recommendations. Over time, the business partner became comfortable with iBAT recommendations, as the numbers were reasonable and better than what their internal system was recommending. In addition, iBAT provided visibility to information not previously available in one convenient tool, such as new product introductions, product transitions, IBM in-house inventory, and reseller inventory. The partner provided valuable feedback, which was used to improve the dashboard and collaboration platform and refine the underlying analytics. In addition, a variety of metrics were developed to monitor the health of the process, such as tracking compliance with recommendations, inventory age, inventory turns, and inventory days of supply (DOS). Figure 3-3 shows an example of a dashboard with "buy" and "sell" recommendations generated by iBAT. Arrow 1 indicates a supply overage, which prompts iBAT to recommend "sell." Arrow 2 indicates an inventory "sell" bringing the actual supply in line with the recommended supply. Arrow 3 shows a buyer bringing inventory in a week early due to a forecasted demand spike. Arrow 4 indicates that on-hand inventory is consumed until it aligns with the sales-out forecast. (To see a color version of this figure, go to http://www.ibmpressbooks.com/title/9780133833034.)

At this stage, the team was ready to move to the next step of production deployment. One of the key lessons learned during the prototype phase was the importance of the business processes in support of analytics. Based on the success of the prototype and confidence in the tool and associated processes, STG management endorsed a change to the IBM channel price protection policy by extending unlimited price protection from previously limited price protection, as long as partners stayed within iBAT recommendations. A regular cadence was developed with the business partners to provide a collaborative exception process, if warranted, and to monitor compliance and channel inventory health.

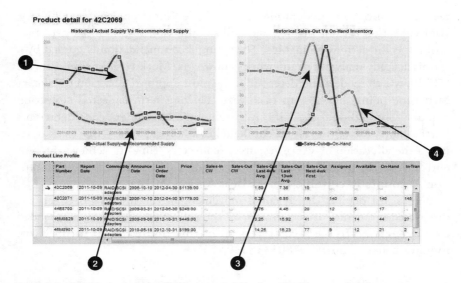

Figure 3-3   IBM Buy Analysis Tool (iBAT)–generated "buy" and "sell" recommendations

Outcome: Reduced Price Protection Expense, Reduced Returns, and Two Industry Awards

iBAT has been very successful. It has reduced price protection expense by 80% and reduced returns by more than 50%. After IBM used and proved the solution internally, it made iBAT available externally as well. iBAT has been recognized by two industry awards: the Tech Data 2010 Inventory Optimization Partner of the Year award and the CRN Channel Champion award in 2010.

Challenge: Improving the Accounts Receivable Business Process and Collector Productivity

As part of optimizing the extended supply chain within IBM, the ISC envisioned a prescriptive analytics solution for the accounts receivable business process. The proposed solution uses predictive analytics and optimization along with smart, dynamic, and flexible rules to recommend specific accounts receivable collection actions, by invoice, globally. Working together with the analytics experts from Research, the team developed a solution that realizes an invoice segmentation strategy based on client payment history, IBM collection actions history, and collection action results history, to prescribe specific actions by invoice. The action recommendation is guided by a sophisticated analytics framework known as Markov Decision Process (MDP), which models and determines the most appropriate action to take, at each time point, in order to maximize the long-term expected collection amount throughout the life of each invoice under consideration.[9] Furthermore, the optimization engine takes a holistic view—that is, it optimizes the allocation of scarce resources (collectors' time) to achieve the best outcome for the overall inventory of receivables. The team dubbed the solution **Accounts Receivable—Next Best Action (NBA)**.

Figure 3-4 depicts the dynamic movement of the invoices between the discovered segments, driven in part by the collection actions recommended by the engine. (To see a color version of this figure, go to http://www. ibmpressbooks.com/title/9780133833034.)

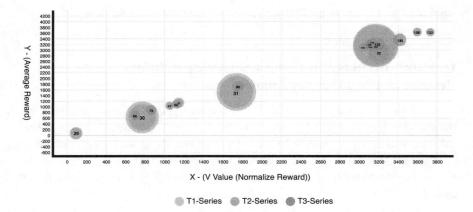

Figure 3-4   Visualization of segment movement for Accounts Receivable—Next Best Action (NBA)

Employing the implementation approach evangelized by O'Sullivan, the team started small by implementing the solution for the U.S. Small and Medium Business operations team. Quickly, the analytics experts and operations team identified improvements in the way the analytics and optimization engine are customized to the specific business process at hand. Although the NBA solution is based on a cutting-edge technology, full automation of a complex business process such as an accounts receivable process will always involve some level of human intervention. In the NBA solution, this is achieved by allowing the users to input their domain knowledge in the form of "prohibition" rules, directing the automated system to "behave" within reasonable bounds considered appropriate in the field, while using the analytics and optimization algorithms within it to optimize the process, subject to the constraints specified by such rules. The analytics and operations teams worked together to carefully formulate these business rules, working to strike a balance between automation and optimization versus respecting the wisdom of the trade embedded in the minds of the experienced collectors. The performance indicators for both the tool and the process were recognized as critical to the success of the project. Alignment of the collectors' performance goals to the new process and tool was identified as an early action and critical success factor, as was the utilization metric. (*Utilization* was defined as the percentage of analytics recommendations executed by the collectors.) The operations, analytics, and project/change management experts worked diligently and collaboratively to continuously improve and expand the scope of the new process and tool, driving significant productivity improvements.

Outcome: Better Visibility to Track the Total Receivables View Across the Entire Collection Process and Reduction in Labor Cost

Today, the implementation continues. Two market-based solutions have been implemented, using the iterative continuous improvement approach. The NBA solution focuses on mature markets that have a rich set of data, as well as a lean, value-based solution for less mature markets with less robust data. In recent months, an increased emphasis on data visualization and dashboards has improved collector utilization. The enhanced insight gives the execution team better visibility to track the total receivables view across the entire collection process. Managers are more effectively monitoring daily debt flow, balancing work load, and prioritizing collectors' focus on any given day. In 2013, a 5.5% reduction in labor cost was realized through the use of the NBA solution.

Challenge: Predicting Disruptions in the Supply Chain

The **Supply Chain Social Listening** project monitors social channels for sentiment and trends that may signal disruptions in the supply chain. This incubator project started as an exploratory collaboration between IBM Research and ISC—with three goals:

- To determine whether social media listening can provide valuable and timely data on events that disrupt the supply chain
- To prove that social media activity for supply chain topics can be captured, reported, and analyzed
- To establish a framework for monitoring social media associated with key events

The Supply Chain Social Listening tool monitors social media sources such as blogs, forums, Twitter, Facebook and LinkedIn, and news feeds to find events that may prevent a supplier from providing services or shipping components to IBM—for example, listening for terms like *power outage* or *strike* in the news feeds from a city of interest. The challenges with social media listening include examining very large volumes of data and dealing with unstructured data. Getting to valuable information and insight often requires iteration. Using IBM Social Media Analytics, a powerful tool for uncovering sentiment across a multitude of online sources, the team works iteratively to pull in data, filter, look at the filtered data, redefine the filter, and so on.

Figure 3-5 shows the steps that the team uses in the social listening project. After collecting the data, the team uses IBM Social Medial Analytics to analyze the social data and generate snippets. Next, the team reviews the snippets. Reports are then generated for review by subject matter experts. Based on the review, the team may start the cycle again. Because the Supply Chain Social Listening project listens to the vast amount of varied social media data and does near real-time analysis, the data has three Vs of big data: *Variety*, *Volume*, and *Velocity*.[10]

Outcome: Number of Listening Events Increased Tenfold and Local Language Listening Proved Valuable

Some initial areas for social listening included supply chain social responsibility, social unrest, and risk. Key findings from the exploratory phase included:

- Activity on economies is typically most reliable and best covered in the mainstream press.

- Riots, demonstrations, and strikes are thoroughly covered in social media, but filtering is required to find this information.
- The mainstream press is best for subject analysis, while social media listening provides insight into sentiment, based on volume.

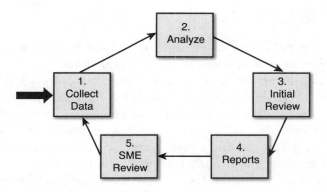

Figure 3-5 Steps to determine sentiment analysis

When the team started, it was listening for only four events. It is now listening for more than 40 events, and it expects the number of events to continue to grow. Supply Chain Social Listening has broadened from focusing on supply chain disruptions to becoming a complementary source to the market intelligence process. The team continues to explore enhanced usage. For example, the team attempted local language listening (in Portuguese) and was impressed to find a mention of a sizable strike at a company in Brazil six days before the Brazilian media reported the strikes; no reports of the strikes were covered in mainstream U.S. media.

Lessons Learned

Analytic solutions are deployed most effectively within the context of business processes. Haye and her team have learned a great deal through the development and deployment of analytics solutions. Haye learned that analytics solutions work best within the context of a business process. The Cross Industry Standard Process for Data Mining (CRISP-DM) defines six phases of analytics projects:[11]

1. Business understanding
2. Data understanding
3. Data preparation
4. Modeling
5. Evaluation
6. Deployment

The "fun math" is typically done is phases 4 and 5. Even though deployment is only one phase, it can be challenging, largely because change is required. Unless a project has a successful deployment phase, providing business results is extremely unlikely. Most of the ISC's analytics applications have had very successful deployments, providing significant results to the business. *A governance model is key to managing an analytics project portfolio.* SSCA has a rigorous and disciplined process for the prioritization, development, and monitoring of all analytic projects within the ISC.

Based on their experiences, Haye and her team have identified three critical success factors for building value through advanced analytics: readiness for change, iterative approach, and incentive alignment. These three criteria are used in project prioritization. The next three paragraphs describe these three critical success factors.

Getting buy-in and readiness for change. SSCA's analytics projects leverage a "three in a box" project approach for effective transformation. Before an analytics project is started, commitment and leadership are required from three areas: the operational execution team, the process transformation team, and the analytics team. The execution team must be willing to change the process to incorporate the analytics results. As critical as the math is, transformation leadership and execution/operations expertise are even more important. Haye has found that 9 times out of 10, the execution team is ready for change, but when it is not, Haye's team stops the project.

Doing things fast is almost always better than doing things perfectly. Unlike traditional IT projects, most analytics projects are exploratory. Building *iteratively* toward a major impact by starting small will yield a much better business result than defining a large and long "big bang" implementation. Getting feedback from each iteration of an analytic project both validates results and allows adjustments to be made before the next iteration. This iterative approach also allows demonstration of improved capabilities along the way, which serves to build progressively stronger stakeholder support, and this approach decreases the time to value.

Aligning incentives contributes to successful deployment and adoption. Designing compelling business benefits for each supply chain participant and reflecting these benefits in terms and conditions aligns incentives, which contributes to successful adoption and deployment of the analytics results. This is a win–win–win for the "three in the box." An interesting example of incentive alignment occurred with the iBAT project. To achieve incentive alignment with trading partners, Haye and her team changed terms and conditions and how, when, and at what level they would pay price protection based on recommendations from the iBAT tool. So the output of the iBAT tool was used to align incentives. You might wonder how executives, each with his or her own objectives, can agree on aligned incentives that are consistent with their objectives. All of the ISC's functional and execution executives are measured on "client first" metrics, as well as other business metrics. Thus, they start off with a fairly balanced, consistent perspective. Haye and her team may optimize a particular element in modeling, but the optimization is always within the bounds acceptable measure—for example, client-acceptable fill rates or serviceability rates. Before deploying operational changes, what-if sensitivity analysis is done to test the impact of the actions.

In addition to the three critical success factors described previously, the ISC learned a lesson about the value of partnering, and three of the analytics solutions described in this chapter are good examples of one of the emerging themes.

Partnering with teams that have deep analytic skills pays off. The ISC has had a long and successful partnership with IBM Research's Math department to develop analytic solutions. Markus Ettl, Senior Manager, Integrated Enterprise Operations Management, has been working on supply chain solutions since he joined IBM in the late 1990s. Ettl was the science lead and project manager for the iBAT solution. He views the ISC as very forward thinking. He believes that partnering with the ISC was effective because he was able to work with people in ISC who had backgrounds similar to his. Ettl starts deploying and making tools available early in a project. This helps convince the stakeholders that there is a path forward and that it is worth investing in the initiative. An analytic solution undergoes several iterations in order to develop the version that ends up in production.

You don't have to understand analytics technology to derive value from it. QEWS, iBAT, and Accounts Receivable—Next Best Action (NBA) are good examples of solutions that have analytics and sophisticated mathematics embedded within them. All three have dashboards that make leveraging the analytics easy to do without requiring an understanding the analytics and optimization used within the solution.

It's important to leverage the levers. As mentioned in Chapter 1, organizations that excel in leveraging the nine levers of differentiation derive the most value from data and analytics.[12] The ISC has a track record of leveraging all nine levers of differentiation that enable organizations to create value from their data. At the *Enable* level, the ISC's analytic solutions have demonstrated sustained business value; their projects include measurement of business outcomes; and their analytic solutions run on several standard platforms, depending on the requirements, so they are leveraging all three levers: *Source of Value, Measurement,* and *Platform.* At the *Drive* level, the ISC has created a strong culture for the availability and use of data and analytics; the CIO has processes that manage the structure and security of supply chain data; and organizational confidence is prevalent in the ISC, which leverages all three levers: *Culture, Data,* and *Trust.* At the *Amplify* level, sponsorship is prevalent in the ISC; SSCA has a strong governance model for funding projects, and it has built up a highly skilled analytics organization that can be leveraged by the ISC, so it is leveraging all three levers: *Sponsorship, Funding,* and *Expertise.*

> *"By using analytics, you learn and get smarter and smarter. Usually, you do not get just one answer, but instead you get a range and then you learn and narrow the range until it becomes more accurate. And it does not stop. You continue to iterate and improve."*
>
> **—Fran O'Sullivan, General Manager, Integrated Supply Chain, IBM Corporation**

IBM's analytics transformation started with the ISC, which has continued to be one of the leading users of analytics within the company. The lessons provided by the use of analytics within the ISC have provided confidence to other business areas as they started their analytics journeys.

Endnotes

1. "Supply Chain Operations Reference (SCOR®) model Overview—Version 10.0," Supply Chain Council, 2010. https://supply-chain.org/f/SCOR-Overview-Web.pdf.
2. Yashchin, E., "Some Aspects of the Theory of Statistical Control Schemes," *IBM Journal of Research and Development*, Volume 31, Number 2, March 1987.

3. Hawkins, D. M., and Olwell, D., "Cumulative Sum Charts and Charting for Quality Improvement," Springer, New York, 1998. http://www.google.com/url?sa=t&rct=j&q=&esrc=s&source=web&cd= 2&ved=0CDAQFjAB&url=http%3A%2F%2Fwww.springer.com%2F productFlyer_978-0-387-98365-3.pdf%3FSGWID%3D0-0-1297- 1515130-0&ei=rfn7UqjBMKvJsQSxpIKgBQ&usg= AFQjCNGEyyh5Q0A7BTxPH4_e3v6yOA9WNA&sig2=pEP77olehy UHW6USxfE8dA&bvm=bv.61190604,d.dmQ.

4. Schroeck, M., et al., "Analytics: The Real-World Use of Big Data: How Innovative Enterprises Extract Value from Uncertain Data," IBM Institute for Business Value, 2012. http://www-03.ibm.com/systems/ hu/resources/the_real_word_use_of_big_data.pdf.

5. *Statistical Quality Control Handbook* (1st ed.), Western Electric Company, Indianapolis, 1956. http://www.worldcat.org/title/statistical-quality-control-handbook/oclc/33858387.

6. "Our 24th Annual Ranking," *Information Week*, September 17, 2012.

7. Ettl, M., and Kapuscinski, R., "Modeling Price Protection Contracts to Improve Distribution Channel Performance in IBM's Extended Server Supply Chain," *Proceedings of the M&SOM Supply Chain Management Conference: Pushing the Frontier—Research Collaborations Between Industry and Academia, Informs*, June 2009.

8. Schroeck, M., et al., "Analytics: The Real-World Use of Big Data."

9. Abe, N., et al., "Optimizing Debt Collections Using Constrained Reinforcement Learning," *Proceedings of the Sixteenth ACM SIGKDD International Conference on Knowledge Discovery and Data Mining*, July 2010. http://www.prem-melville.com/publications/constrained-reinforcement-learning-kdd2010.pdf.

10. Schroeck, M., et al., "Analytics: The Real-World Use of Big Data."

11. Chapman, P., et al., "CRISP-DM 1.0: Step-by-Step Data Mining Guide," SPSS, Inc., 2000. ftp://ftp.software.ibm.com/software/analytics/spss/support/Modeler/Documentation/14/UserManual/CRISP-DM.pdf.

12. Balboni, F., et al., "Analytics: A Blueprint for Value—Converting Big Data and Analytics Insights into Results," IBM Institute of Business Value, 2013. http://public.dhe.ibm.com/common/ssi/ecm/en/gbe03575usen/GBE03575USEN.PDF.

4

Anticipating the
Financial Future

"Our success is going to depend at the end of the day on how we continuously transform and change our skills. Only then, when we transform our skills and expertise from basic gathering and reporting data to really providing predictive analytics and business insight, can we deliver on our trusted business advisor role."

—James Kavanaugh, Vice President and Controller, IBM Corporation

Perspective: Big Data and Analytics
Increase Value of Finance Team

Historically, finance organizations have been expected to report business performance in an accurate, structured, timely way, from quarterly earnings to annual reports. Now forecasting is becoming a more important part of the finance "DNA," and analytics skills are highly valued. While reporting remains a core competency, much more is being expected of finance organizations as firms seek to anticipate the future. The role of finance, particularly the CFO position, is undergoing a significant transformation as finance is being asked to produce better business insights that leads to better outcomes.

Finance organizations use big data and analytics to generate insights (sometimes referred to as "headlights") for the business in ways that were previously not possible. This evolution elevates the role of finance to a trusted business partner, working across the organization to influence strategy and maximize business performance. Analytics enables a finance organization's activities to become more predictive in nature and allows the organization to anticipate the future with greater accuracy.

Within IBM, the Finance organization operates as a shared service supporting all of IBM's operations globally. This structure has developed over a number of years, replacing the previously fragmented support that was directly aligned to individual business units. The role of Finance has evolved over the past decade, with analytics playing a growing role in the transformed function. Even though Finance is one of the leading groups within IBM in the use of analytics, it has only just begun to tap into the potential that big data and analytics offer. This is a story of how an organization has transformed to capitalize on the value of analytics and has taken proactive steps to drive the necessary culture change to enable it.

IBM's Finance organization faced many challenges during this transformation. In the 1990s, it was highly decentralized and operated a maze of separate accounting, measurement, and reporting systems. It had twice as many employees as the finance organizations of IBM's competitors yet was only able to provide limited information to report detailed business results. It spent a large percentage of time and skilled labor on administrative tasks. The combination of a lack of integration and a proliferation of unique measurement systems led to inconsistent data. Not surprisingly, the business units viewed the 1990s Finance function at IBM as adding minimal value. Analytics has opened up a world of opportunities for Finance to increase its value to the business.

Getting the Basics in Place

Peter Hayes, IBM Director of Business Analytics and Finance IT, says that one of the foundational steps taken early in this transformation was to ensure conformance to a common chart of accounts so that accountants and planners around the world were all creating financial data consistently. The Finance transformation journey had to begin with a strong focus on foundational items such as common processes, systems, and data standards. It would later build on that foundation with predictive analytics, prescriptive analytics, and optimization. Importantly, the organization did not wait until it had "perfect data" to start using analytics but instead began to derive value from the existing available data. Figure 4-1 shows how the disparate data collected, country by country, was preventing an effective holistic view of key performance indicators across the enterprise.

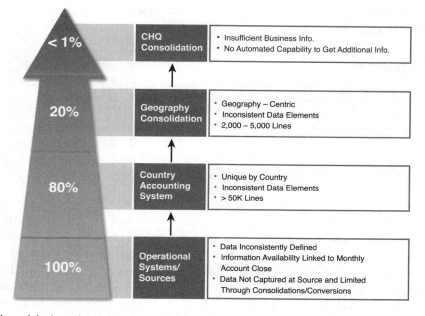

Figure 4-1 Inconsistent data shows vital information loss at each consolidation level

When asked to describe how its analytic journey began, the Finance organization had difficulty answering. Finance, by its very nature, has been doing analysis for years. As new data and computational capabilities became available, Finance built on the quantitative nature of its culture to increase the use of analytics and embed it into its business processes. In 2013, research published in the article "Analytics: A Blueprint for Value" highlighted the importance of the right alignment of strategy, technology, and organizational structure.[1] The Finance organization has taken steps that leverage each of the nine levers over the course of its transformation—*Culture, Data, Expertise, Funding, Measurement, Platform, Source of Value, Sponsorship,* and *Trust.*

Creating an Analytics Culture

Finance has taken several proactive steps to create an analytics culture. In 2009, the Finance leadership team kicked off a project to drive awareness of the power of business analytics throughout the finance community. This led to the creation of the Finance Leadership Advocacy Group (FLAG) to promote the use of analytics. FLAG's mission was to lead the adoption of business analytics across Finance, educate and drive awareness of the power of business analytics, and set the agenda and prioritize investments in business analytics (see Figure 4-2).

FLAG Mission:
- Lead the Adoption of Business Analytics
- Educate and Drive Awareness of the Power of Business Analytics
- Set the Agenda and Prioritize Investments

Assigned Ownership

Business Prioritization
Benefits Realization
Finance Culture
Communication
Education

Figure 4-2 The Finance Leadership Advocacy Group (FLAG) helps drive the use of analytics in Finance

IBM's Finance leadership drives culture change through the Finance organization and holds Finance to a higher standard through the innovative use of tools such as the Analytics Quotient (http://www-01.ibm.com/ software/analytics/aq/). IBM Controller James Kavanaugh has also taken steps to educate all the Finance managers about the "art of the possible" with analytics, making it clear that this is the future of Finance at IBM. Understanding how to leverage analytics will enable the organization to be at the forefront of strategy development and company performance. The stakes are high, and Finance has a clear direction, supported by the training needed to leverage this competitive advantage. It is a very pragmatic move to drive better business outcomes. This is not doing analytics for the sake of analytics but is core and fundamental to what Finance does.

A key initiative was an event held in fall 2012, when all IBM's Finance managers from around the globe were brought together, using Livestream video, for a half-day education session designed to improve their understanding of big data and analytics and the value they can drive. This meeting empowered attendees to infuse analytics within their decision processes to drive more fact-based decision making. Carlos Passi, Assistant Controller, Business Transformation, brought in experts from across the enterprise to showcase and explore inspiring use cases. A powerful culmination of the session was the Analytics Quotient quiz results. Kavanaugh challenged his management team to increase the prevalence of analytics throughout the function and issued a call to action to do so. This engagement and sponsorship demonstrate one of the key elements of a successful analytic journey: a high level of support within the organization. It helped establish the strategic intent of data and analytics investments, using measurable business outcomes.[2] Kavanaugh was able to create explicit connections between Finance's goals and the analytics activities showcased. The transformation of the Finance organization is illustrative of the journey to using more fact-based analytics within business processes.

A further example of senior leadership support came at the worldwide Finance Town Hall meeting held early in 2013. Mark Loughridge, Senior Vice President and Chief Financial Officer, issued a challenge to members of the worldwide Finance team to generate innovative ideas on how Finance can drive business benefits through the use of analytics. Entries would be judged on innovation, business value, and value to the Finance organization, and a winning team would be selected each quarter. This is another tangible example of working the *Culture* and *Sponsorship* levers in an organization.

Challenge: Improving Efficiency and Effectiveness of Managing Worldwide Spending

IBM Finance leverages analytics in three key areas: to drive operational efficiency, to manage risk, and to provide business insight. Each of these areas is illustrated here with specific examples.

Tracking Spending: The Worldwide Spend Project

IBM needed to more efficiently and effectively track worldwide expenses and provide the capability to drill down into spending details by specific geographic areas. Creating one global repository for all the spending management system information was a significant undertaking.

Data is often a big challenge in analytics projects. For the **Worldwide Spend** project, the financial data already existed in the ledger, which was the trusted source. However, ensuring consistent data definitions and consistent rules for classifying ledger entries as spend was necessary.

The data model used IBM Cognos® TM1® as a repository. The challenge was to reduce 18 cubes to a single cube and to be able to add more dimensions and more data to that cube, with no loss of responsiveness compared to using the 18 separate cubes. (A *cube* is a set of data organized by dimensions and measures for the purpose of aggregating different subsets of the larger set of data. For example, a cube of sales data might provide aggregations of the same data by product, by time, or by sales region dimensions. Looking at the cube enables you to view the total sales of a product, within a business region, during a particular fiscal quarter.) The team was able to accomplish this goal and phase out the use of other cubes. The single cube provided the basis for both the predictive analytics and harmonized reporting elements of the project. The project is being ported to IBM's SPSS® Modeler in order to take advantage of an increased number of algorithms and factors such as seasonality.

While working on the Worldwide Spend project, stakeholders were engaged early, and the team took a simple approach to getting stakeholder and leader buy-in: listening. They took the time to ask questions and listen carefully to the stakeholder responses. What is most important? What are you missing today? What would make you more effective? From those discussions, the team focused on building in that capability. But it did not stop there. The team went all the way down to the user level and asked the same questions. As in many analytics projects, they found disconnects between objectives at one level and constraints (or supposed requirements) at another level, between what was being done and why it was being done. For example, a user said, "I have to produce this because my CFO requires it." The team went back to the CFO, and he said, "No, I don't ever look at that; I don't know what it is used for." The team discovered that over time, assumptions had become entrenched in the process. Listening to all of the stakeholders, making sure that the necessary data and analysis were understood at all levels, and providing clarity on the project requirements and plans were critical to the success of transformational analytics. Throughout the project, key stakeholders were updated on progress—both what was going well and what was not—so plans could be put in place to quickly recover when necessary.

With the foundational elements of Worldwide Spend in place, the door was open for additional applications. One requirement was to enable head-count reporting in a similar format—pulling data from trusted sources, based on consistent definitions and tied to other numbers used to manage the business. The next step was to use this data foundation for predictive analytics, which transformed the forecasting approach for spending.

The predictive portion of the Worldwide Spend project forecasts spending. These forecasts are required quickly, often within one or two days. To achieve this velocity, the analytics team chose financial analysts who had the best track records to examine what techniques were used. Through that inquiry, it was determined that most of the best analysts were using some type of simple regression, using past performance to predict the future. The analytics team included regression methods in its model and added additional methods (16 algorithms in all) as well as logic that can recommend for an analyst which algorithm to select for a particular forecast. The Worldwide Spend solution delivers these 16 algorithmic approaches in seconds and offers an analyst more options than the few that were used before. Providing the user with both familiar tools and more sophisticated methods, offering recommendations, and allowing the user to compare the results of different methods helped to build user confidence in new tools.

Education also played an important role in the acceptance of the solution. The model gave financial analysts override capability, based on material events. Initially there were cases in which an analyst would override each element in the model. This presented an opportunity for the team to engage with the analyst to learn what the material event was. The team found that sometimes analysts didn't understand the algorithms and reverted to what they knew. One reason analysts cited for returning to old methods was that they felt comfortable explaining the old methods and did not want to simply tell their managers that "the model said so" when describing a forecast. Once the analysts understood the algorithms, they trusted the model and became more confident when presenting the results to their leadership team. The use of overrides then decreased, and the power of the models was used in the forecasting process. Because they were comfortable with their old methods and being asked to change, the financial analysts in this example required a deeper understanding of the technology and algorithms than is typical of users. This is in contrast to the users described in Chapter 3, "Optimizing the Supply Chain," who made very effective use of analytics models embedded in solutions without having to understand the underlying analytics technology.

The Finance team used a systematic approach and measured progress in several ways. On the predictive part of the project, Finance demonstrated that the model was at least as accurate as the previously used methods and that analysts' time was freed up to do deeper analytics to bring more insights to the business. One measure used with the leadership team was simply asking, "Are you getting better information now?"

Outcome: More Efficient and More Effective Spend Forecasting

The Worldwide Spend project provided the holistic view needed to inform business decisions on spending. This project provides a data foundation that supports further analytics initiatives. In addition, the team found that process simplification supporting the deployment of Worldwide Spend improved employee retention. It is easier to retain the best analysts and talent if they are working on predictive models and developing algorithms, talking to people about the use and impact of analytics, and adding insight for the business to act on. That type of work is much more interesting than gathering data to fill in reports.

Challenge: Improving Productivity and Accuracy While Minimizing Risk in Tax and Statutory Reporting

Most enterprises are challenged to keep up with frequently changing tax and statutory reporting requirements.

Keeping Up with Reporting Requirements: The Accelerated External Reporting (AER) System

One of the challenges of operating in more than 170 countries is keeping up with the tax and statutory reporting requirements in those locations. The Finance organization knew it would improve productivity and accuracy while minimizing risk if the data was collected in a common global system for financial consolidation, reporting, and analytics. This solution also provided an opportunity for IBM to automate the mapping of Generally Accepted Accounting Principles (GAAP) to local statutory reporting standards (using International Finance Reporting Standards [IFRS] as a common baseline) and to strategically position itself to support regulatory changes such as using XBRL for external reporting.

Like other multinational corporations, IBM risks fines and stock price impacts if its non-U.S. reporting is inaccurate. The **Accelerated External Reporting (AER)** system addresses all the country-specific rules and requirements for doing business outside the United States. It manages all the financial reporting components, ensures that the rules are applied correctly, and provides a clear and accurate financial message.

IBM Accounting anticipates significant productivity savings through the application of the AER system. As with Worldwide Spend, a common process and a common system eliminate multiple tools and spreadsheets and time-consuming manual reconciliations.

The AER solution also showcases IBM's own technologies. Utilizing Cognos TM1 for data consolidation, Cognos Business Intelligence (BI) for standardized internal reports, and Cognos Disclosure Management (CDM) for formal reporting, the teams have furthered the development and marketability of IBM's software products.

The IBM AER solution brings together capabilities for data collection, analytic data management, review and approval, and disclosure preparation and distribution. It enables Finance teams to collect data for tax reporting and regulatory disclosure and perform mapping from GAAP to local reporting standards. Finance can now perform what-if scenarios on any and all of the data collected and map it to a data warehouse to be able to drill down for details. This solution is used within IBM and is now available commercially as well.

Outcome: Improved Statutory and Tax Reporting and Analytics

This example drove significant benefit for IBM by creating an asset that not only improved its internal processes but could also be made available externally to help IBM's clients with their tax and statutory reporting. The solution streamlines data gathering and external reporting for both statutory and tax environments. It shifts financial analysts' efforts from collecting the data to analyzing the data for insights. It eliminates manual work and inconsistent collection of data and supports deep-dive analytics that were not possible when the data existed in separate spreadsheets owned and managed by separate organizations. It has the potential to save millions of dollars annually on staffing, consultancy, and auditing for statutory reporting.

Challenge: Balancing Risk and Reward

How can a global company operating in multiple countries stay on top of information and events in order to figure out where to invest, how to allocate capital, and how to manage cash in different regions? IBM faces such a challenge with operations in more than 170 countries; understanding and gaining foresight into the changing worldwide markets is a key objective.

Assessing Risk: Country Financial Risk Scorecard

To get a better handle on country-level business performance, IBM created the **Country Financial Risk Scorecard**, an automated tool and methodology that leverages IBM SPSS Modeler.

The business challenge was threefold:

n   Provide a consistent approach, tools, and methodology for quantifying and prioritizing financial risks in the various countries where IBM operates n Use an integrated, consolidated, and actionable platform for the global user community

n Expand capabilities through the statistical ability of the available tools

The Country Financial Risk Scorecard uses big data and analytics to provide IBM with insight into key risk and performance indicators in four categories: economic indicators, financial or shareholder value indicators, liquidity factors, and risk reward. The Country Financial Risk Scorecard monitors hundreds of macroeconomic inputs, including currency fluctuations, shifts in regulatory environment, socioeconomic conditions, and growth patterns. Figure 4-3 highlights key categories of information used to assess a risk score. With this scorecard, IBM can look at historical-based performance reporting by country in each one of these areas and leverage that information for predictive analysis, scenario modeling, and stress testing. This insight enables Finance to make more informed decisions about investment prioritization, capital allocation, and cash management.

Country Financial Risk Scorecard

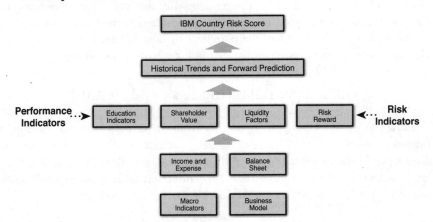

Figure 4-3 The Country Financial Risk Scorecard uses big data and analytics to assess risk

The Country Financial Risk Scorecard is built on IBM technology. IBM SPSS Modeler is used to calculate the IBM country risk score, integrating all inputs and applying mathematical algorithms to provide scores in each category. The average of these risk scores is the total risk score. Future risk scores are predicted using time-series forecasting for the next three months.

Outcome: Country Financial Risk Scorecard Uses Big Data to Monitor Trends and Minimize Risk

The Country Financial Risk Scorecard has provided significant value to the business by creating near real-time views of risk for 170 countries. Figure 4-4 shows sample output based on a point-in-time financial risk assessment. The visualization uses three shades of color coding to differentiate risk profile for that time. (To see a color version of this figure, go to http://www.ibmpressbooks.com/title/9780133833034.)

Figure 4-4   A sample heatmap that visually displays a point-in-time financial risk profile

This project was recognized by *CIO* magazine and profiled as a CIO 100 Award winner in 2012 for innovation and leadership. One example of a significant outcome occurred when the model was able to predict a currency loss exposure from investments in a country that was faltering. IBM was able to take mitigating actions to deliver a better outcome.

Challenge: Validating Acquisition Strategy

Identifying potential acquisitions and supporting integration is an essential element of IBM's growth strategy. IBM invested $39 billion in acquisitions between 2000 and 2013. IBM spent more than $17 billion on acquisitions for business analytics and optimization alone between 2005 and 2013.

Managing M & A: The Mergers and Acquisitions Analytics Project

With an extensive list of acquisitions, the **Mergers and Acquisitions Analytics** project was undertaken to learn from those experiences in order to predict which projects would be most likely to succeed in the future. Paul Price, IBM Director of Mergers and Acquisitions Integration, said this is not a big data application; it uses a modest amount of data with very sophisticated analytics to predict future risk associated with portfolio strategy.

An acquisition, like any other investment, requires a business plan detailing expenses to be incurred and revenue to be realized. An acquisition can fail to meet a business plan for a variety of reasons, including business model conflicts, clashing corporate cultures, and delays in integration. Having some level of visibility in terms of how the acquisition is likely to perform would help IBM manage risk and optimize acquisition performances. This is where analytics comes into play.

Acquisitions represent an important way for IBM to expand its portfolio offerings and tap into new markets. IBM's acquisitions strategy now leverages analytics to identify potential acquisition candidates and support integration activities. When an acquisition candidate is identified, the model assesses the candidate with the 18 key attributes identified as critical to achieving the acquisition's business case. See Figure 4-5 for an example assessment of 18 key attributes of the Mergers and Acquisitions Analytics project. The use of analytics to support the strategy has proven to be a game changer for IBM. Analytics has helped identify the sweet spot for acquisitions.

Outcome: Mergers and Acquisitions Analytics Improves Success Rate

IBM has been able to use what it has learned from historical acquisitions to predict the likelihood of success with potential acquisitions. The investment in the Mergers and Acquisitions Analytics project since 2010 is indicative of the value being realized; IBM's acquisition portfolio performance is ahead of the industry.

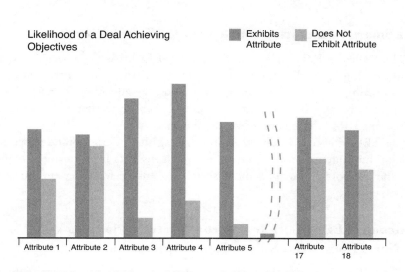

Figure 4-5 Mergers and Acquisitions Analytics assesses 18 key attributes

The field of mergers and acquisitions is dynamic, and the Mergers and Acquisitions Analytics model continues to be refined as data from new acquisitions is incorporated. Deal types change over time, so the usual "repeat, learn, refine" approach cannot be directly applied here. The model assists with the decision process of evaluating options—not simply A or B but optimizing between A and B. It supports top-down strategy by aiding in the assessment of organic versus inorganic approaches to fill gaps in IBM's product portfolio. It is designed for an expert user to provide fact-based assessments and insights to inform strategy and decisions. The model develops the information, and the expert user adds the subject matter expertise and provides advice for the business in addition to tracking acquisition performance to identify which indicators need to be most closely monitored to ensure success.

Price says, "I've learned the people who are best at unlocking the real potential here are not the pure-play finance person or the pure-play analytics modeler but the individuals who have an understanding of each. The people who can build a hypothesis, mine data, visualize the data, and apply creative thinking to solve the business problem. It takes time to learn those dimensions but is well worth the investment." Price recommends learning the theory and mastering the application of elements such as portfolio theory to form a solid foundation along with analytics skills.

The Smarter Enterprise Enablement (SEE) Initiative

The Smarter Enterprise Enablement (SEE) Initiative integrates data, business logic, and analytical modeling within a central system. Transforming a strategic planning process to take advantage of analytics to improve outcomes is a significant challenge, and one that IBM Research helped the IBM Finance organization take on.

The SEE project is intended to improve agility in cross-brand processes, develop intelligence to inform decisions with insights from business analytics, and support the management system to ensure focus on the business objectives.

Outcome: SEE Project Transforms Strategic Planning and Its Novel Approach Leads to Patent Applications

The SEE tool enables the team to model and analyze the impact of different assumptions on the business through the use of what-if scenarios. Using an analytic model allows for quick evaluation of a what-if scenario—requiring far less time than manual calculations. For example, a team can run revenue scenarios and assess the pipeline and determine whether it is optimistic or realistic. The multipurpose capabilities of SEE include sensitivity analysis and uncertainty analysis. SEE also helps connect financial and operational requirements and objectives. The white paper "Enterprise Transformation: An Analytics-Based Approach to Strategic Planning" describes both the models and building the capability to transform the strategic planning process to leverage analytics throughout.[3]

The work and novelty of the SEE approach led to the filing of a number of patent applications.

What's Next for IBM Finance?

The next wave of transformation for IBM Finance is to raise the organization's Analytics Quotient (AQ), which measures readiness to use analytics to garner insight, influence decision making, and automate processes. IBM Finance has established a 2015 Analytics Quotient goal that will take the organization to higher AQ levels. Its goal is for 90% of the population to recognize the organization as performing at stage three (leader) or stage four (master) by 2015. The evolution depicted in Figure 4-6 is being fueled by analytics, and Finance has positioned itself well to leverage the capabilities.

Figure 4-6 The evolving role of Finance, fueled by big data and analytics

Doug Dow, Vice President, IBM Business Analytics Transformation, sees what the IBM Finance team is doing to use analytics and make it part of their business practices as a great example for the rest of IBM. Dow said, "Analytics is a way of doing business. It's not just a set of technologies. The IBM Finance organization has embraced this approach as a way to improve how they do business, as well as the results that the business produces."

Lessons Learned

Transformation requires strong executive support, clear targets, and measurable objectives. The strong executive support and investment in raising the awareness and understanding of the possibilities that big data and analytics offer was pivotal to driving the culture change for the Finance organization.

Effective transformation requires a focus on data, processes, and tools. Transformation is difficult, and doing it right requires a focus not just on the data or tools but also on the processes. The three-pronged approach was very beneficial to Finance. As Peter Hayes has said, *"We will never be done."* Transformation is a continuous effort that requires dedicated resources to get results. As analytics informs decision processes, it is critical to engage employees to drive adoption.

Using analytics leads to better auditability and accountability. With the use of analytics, the decision-making process becomes more structured and repeatable, and a decision becomes less dependent on the individual making it. When people change positions, things still happen in the same way. You can often go back and find out what analysis was used and why a decision was made.

It's important to leverage the levers. Finance has been actively engaging on all three levels of value impact among the nine levers outlined in "Analytics: A Blueprint for Value" and discussed in Chapter 1, "Why Big Data and Analytics?"[4] Finance has taken proactive steps with the *Enable* levers to form the basis for using big data and analytics to differentiate performance; the *Drive* levers to drive the adoption of the projects and realize value; and the *Amplify* levers to boost the ability to create value from data analytics. The Mergers and Acquisitions Analytics project has boosted the value created through improving the performance of the acquisitions portfolio.

Through a strong focus on each of these levers, the Finance organization has taken innovative steps to enable the use of analytics and drive the needed culture change so that value will not only be realized but also amplified as Finance scales solutions across geographies.

Endnotes

1. Balboni, F., et al., "Analytics: A Blueprint for Value—Converting Big Data and Analytics Insights into Results," IBM Institute for Business Value, 2013. http://public.dhe.ibm.com/common/ssi/ecm/en/gbe03575usen/GBE03575USEN.PDF.
2. Ibid., p. 19.
3. Kapoor, S., et al., "Enterprise Transformation: An Analytics-Based Approach to Strategic Planning," *IBM Journal of Research and Development*, Volume 56, Number 6, November/December 2012. http://ieeexplore.ieee.org/stamp/stamp.jsp?tp=&arnumber=6353948&isnumber=6353928.
4. Balboni, F., et al., "Analytics: A Blueprint for Value."

5

Enabling Analytics Through Information Technology

"It's critical for CIOs in public- and private-sector organizations to turn the huge volumes of data being amassed across the enterprise into insights and to turn those insights into competitive advantage for the business."

—Jeanette Horan, Vice President and Chief Information Officer, IBM Corporation

Perspective: Applying Analytics to IT and Enabling Big Data and Analytics Across an Enterprise

Analytics and customers are on the mind of many chief information officers (CIOs). In a 2011 survey, "The Essential CIO: Insights from the Global Chief Information Officer Study," 83% of CIOs said they had plans that include using business intelligence and analytics to increase competitiveness, and 95% of CIOs said they had plans to lead or support efforts to take advantage of analytics to drive better real-time decisions.[1] While most CIOs' plans included use of analytics, there were striking differences in the surveyed population. CIOs generally spend part of their time on IT fundamentals, but beyond this, four distinct mandates emerged:

- **Expand:** Refine business processes and enhance collaboration
- **Leverage:** Streamline operations
- **Transform:** Change industry value chain
- **Pioneer:** Radically innovate products and markets

The needs of the enterprise largely determine which of these four mandates is primary for its CIO: Seventy percent of the CIOs with Transform as their primary mandate have a priority to turn data into information and information into business insight, and most of these CIOs will focus on a range of tools to drive better decision making over the next five years.[2]

A 2013 study, "The Customer-Activated Enterprise: Insights from the Global C-Suite Study," also found that CIOs are looking outside the enterprise to generate new value.[3] A major shift in the priorities of the IT function is expected over the next few years. More time is expected to be spent on customer experience management and new business development. More than four-fifths of CIOs who responded plan to support marketing by focusing their IT activities in two areas: using analytics to create deep insight from structured and unstructured data and improving their understanding of customers through the use of technologies, processes, and tools.

The CIO organization plays two roles with respect to big data and analytics in an enterprise. First, the CIO organization is a consumer of analytics. In this role, CIO organizations have many opportunities to leverage big data and analytics to support the IT function. Big data and analytics can be used to reduce cost, improve service, and provide function. The second role that a CIO organization plays is to enable the transformation of an enterprise through the use of analytics in multiple dimensions:

- When a CIO organization develops enterprise-wide applications that leverage big data and perform analytics, the enterprise's employees become consumers of big data and analytics.
- The CIO is also in a good position to develop an enterprise-wide information strategy and execute processes for governance and security of data.
- CIO organizations can partner with business teams to develop analytic solutions.

- Setting up a robust infrastructure can be daunting for those new to analytics. CIO organizations can provide an infrastructure comprised of software for data preparation and analytics software for use across the enterprise.

IBM's CIO organization has played a significant role in enabling IBM's transformation to a smarter enterprise through the use of big data and analytics. But before we explore this role, let's look at a few examples of how IBM's CIO organization has used big data and analytics to improve the function of IT.

Challenge: Deciding When to Modernize Servers

Analytics can be used to reduce cost of server modernization and improve service. Deciding when to modernize the hardware and software of servers is often done manually, based on experience or simple business rules such as "upgrade every four years." Modernization actions include operating system refresh; hardware refresh; CPU, memory, or disk capacity increase; and virtualization. Because medium- to large-sized companies typically have many servers in their infrastructure (often more than 5,000), an approach for the modernization of servers that upgrades them near, but before, the time of failure lowers costs and improves service.

IBM's IT operations staff teamed with IBM Research to develop a novel, automated approach for determining optimal application modernization actions for servers, based on actual individual server behavior.[4] The solution was named **Predictive Analytics for Server Incident Reduction (PASIR)**. The prevailing wisdom was that the causes of incidents were old hardware, outdated operating systems, and heavy usage; however, the team could not prove that these items themselves were statistically significant predictors of incidents. Instead, they found that there was a statistically significant interaction among the three items. As the team investigated further, it created a random forest model of the interaction of the terms to classify the servers and, from this classification, predict failure. The random forest model is used to determine whether the number of incident tickets for the server exceeds a threshold, and if it does, the server is classified as problematic. Monte Carlo simulation is used to evaluate and rank modernization choices to help identify the optimal modernization action.

Outcome: Increase in Application Availability

Figure 5-1 shows box plots before and after server refresh. A box plot is a graphical tool that can be used to compare performance before and after a process change. For each box, the bottom of the box is the 25th percentile of the data, and the top of the box is the 75th percentile of the data. In box plots, the median (the middle value when the data is sorted by magnitude) is represented by the line within each the box. In Figure 5-1, the black dots are UNIX® servers, and the white dots are Intel® servers. You can see from this figure that the number of incident tickets per server and per month goes down after refresh. The maximum number of tickets per server and per month decreases from about 5 to about 2. The median decreases from about 0.3 to nearly 0. In this case, the use of this predictive model resulted in a sevenfold increase in application availability. (To see a color version of this figure, go to http://www.ibmpressbooks.com/title/9780133833034.)

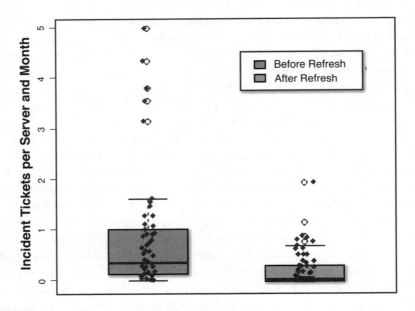

Figure 5-1   Using box plots to visualize the impact of server refresh

As described in Chapter 1, "Why Big Data and Analytics?" using one or more of the nine levers of differentiation increases the value an organization realizes from its data.[5] The use of analytics to optimize server modernization actions is an example of the *Source of Value* lever of differentiation.

Challenge: Detecting Security Incidents

Security is an IT function to which big data and analytics can be applied with valuable results. Security data can be used to analyze activities and metrics associated with risk management, incident detection/response, regulatory compliance, and investigations/forensics. In the past, IBM's IT Risk organization had many security products deployed. Each product has its own console, data sources, and reports. Cross-correlation between the different data sources typically happened only when people got together to discuss a particular security incident. IT Risk was missing *systematic* cross-correlation of security data sources, which meant some security anomalies were likely not being detected. The IT Risk organization needed an integrated solution for big data security analytics and selected IBM QRadar® Security Intelligence Platform, software to detect and defend against network security threats. This product was developed by Q1 Labs®, which IBM acquired in 2011. Many data sources are fed into QRadar and are parsed in real time, using a set of rules to detect security anomalies; this data has two of the four big data Vs: *Volume* and *Velocity*.[6] Using the output from QRadar, a security analyst creates a detailed view of a security anomaly, which includes the rules that triggered it and what the analytics found. This view is then passed on to the security incident response team for handling.

Outcome: Increased Detection of Security Incidents

By using QRadar to cross-correlate security data sources, IT Risk is able to detect threats that would have otherwise been missed. The use of big data and analytics to detect and defend against network security threats is an example of the *Source of Value* lever of differentiation.[7]

Enabling the Transformation to a Smarter Enterprise

Now let's look at the much bigger role that a CIO organization can play— namely enabling the transformation to a smarter enterprise.

Developing Enterprise-Wide Big Data and Analytics Applications

One dimension of the role that IBM's CIO organization plays is the development of multiple enterprise-wide applications that leverage big data and analytics. A good example of the effectiveness of the CIO as a channel for use of big data and analytics is **Faces**, an application that radically improves people search within IBM.[8] Faces has a simple, intuitive interface. Users simply type in what they know about the person (or persons) they are looking for, such as first name, location, and skill. As the user is typing, Faces presents and updates results, searching across all content in the user's profile and taking into account phonetic misspellings. Using an approach similar to that used by the Watson *Jeopardy!* computer,[9] Faces analyzes a large amount of data to select multiple results matching a Faces search, which is an example of one of the four big data Vs: *Volume*.[10] After Faces finds matches, it scores the candidates, bringing the most relevant results to the top. A goal of Faces is to provide results very quickly. This is achieved by a massive-scale back end that precalculates and stores information. Faces has been rapidly adopted within IBM and is extremely popular. Many IBM employees have a browser tab reserved for Faces and use it many times a day. Users of Faces do not have to understand the data sources or the matching analysis or the scoring algorithm; they simply reap the rewards of a simple, fast, and effective people search tool. Faces is a good example of two of the nine levers of differentiation for realizing value from data:[11] *Culture*, because it makes available the use of data and analytics within IBM, and *Source of Value*, since it generates results (that is, an effective people search).

As previously noted, transformation (getting people to change) can be very challenging. When enterprise-wide applications leverage analytics and big data to intuitively produce a speedy result that is superior to results provided from other tools (such as people search tools), people change quickly, and everyone wins.

An emerging and much more ambitious analytics and big data application is **Watson Sales Assistant**, which is based on Watson technology[12] and attacks a more difficult problem than playing *Jeopardy!*—namely providing answers to questions sellers have about the more than 2,000 software and hardware products and thousands more service offerings. Today, sellers spend hours looking through up to a dozen large repositories in a variety of formats to try to find the information they need. Watson ingests the data from these repositories, which is an example of two of the four big data Vs: *Volume* and *Variety*.[13] Using Watson technology, users ask a question. Watson Sales Assistant uses the context it knows about the user, about the products and offerings, and about clients to determine the answers the seller is looking for by searching vast amounts of internal content including IBM Connections, IBM's internal website, sales databases, and asset databases, as well as external content on ibm.com, selecting plausible answers, scoring the answers, and presenting the answers with the highest scores first. Like Faces, Watson

Sales Assistant is a good example of two of the nine levers of differentiation for realizing value from data:[14] *Culture*, because it makes available the use of data and analytics within IBM, and *Source of Value*, since it quickly provides needed content.

Partnering with Business Areas to Develop Social Media Analytic Solutions for Customer-Centric Outcomes

Several years ago, to jump-start IBM's transformation to a customer-centric enterprise, Jeanette Horan, Vice President and Chief Information Officer of IBM, created a team of social media analytics (SMA) experts to partner with business teams enterprise-wide to develop customer-centric solutions. The team's Social & Text Analytics offering, which includes using their infrastructure for SMA, has been used by dozens of organizations across IBM. Some examples include monitoring social activity about "Social Business"; detecting leakage of confidential information; and determining sentiment, volume, and influencers for IBM products. Using a team of SMA experts to partner with the business on customer-centric projects is an example of two of the nine levers of differentiation for realizing value from data:[15] *Expertise*, since the partnering with SMA experts increases SMA skill, and *Platform*, since the SMA team uses its SMA infrastructure for the projects.

Developing an Information Agenda and Processes for Governance and Security of Data

CIOs agree with chief marketing officers (CMOs) that data investments are a high priority and identify five activities to get insight from both structured and unstructured data: master data management, analytics for client outcomes, data warehouses, dashboards, and search capabilities.[16]

However, there is a caution with master data management and data warehouses. What to do with data and when to do it is a controversial subject. In past years, building data warehouses prior to starting BI projects was popular. Once a data warehouse is complete, the data is cleansed, complete, organized, and ready to use, which simplifies life for a BI professional. The downside of this approach is that building a data warehouse can take considerable time—so much time that the business requirements for the data may change before the data warehouse is complete. Instead of building data warehouses, we recommend that an information agenda—a high-level plan, driven by business needs—be developed to guide data preparation work in an iterative fashion. As the business needs change, they can be reflected in the information agenda. The CIO is in a good position to collect data requirements for analytics projects from the business functions and to use these requirements to develop an enterprise-wide information agenda.

So, where did IBM start? To minimize time to value, IBM chose to have the business functions drive individual information agendas, which allowed the business challenges to determine which data needed to be governed, cleansed, and prepared. After several years of targeted but fragmented data activity, moving to an enterprise view offers value, such as cost savings through shared use of common data. IBM's journey to improve internal data has been under way for multiple years. In the past several years, data activities have been focused on accelerating the convergence and consolidation opportunities within the data landscape to better optimize for analytics and operational effectiveness. In 2011, the CIO organization began inventorying IBM's existing structured data sources and constructed an end-state vision for what the data landscape should be. More recently, the CIO organization started assessing the trust for approximately 200 master data stores. The next step, starting with the data that the business functions need most, is to begin data cleansing and centralization to make the data more accessible for analytics.

IBM has five types of trusted data sources that are fed from approximately 200 master data stores:

- More than 25 **transactional data stores** are the original source of the transactional data.

- More than 25 **operation data stores** get data from the originating source in near real time.

- Approximately 50 **data/information warehouses** get data from the originating source or the operation data stores; they contain historical and derived data.

- More than 100 (and counting) **data marts** support specific needs of user communities.

- A large number of **information delivery front ends** provide data for reporting and dashboard needs.

Figure 5-2 illustrates the relationship between the master data stores and the five types of trusted data sources.

These data sources are *transactional*—that is, they are data about customer transactions, such as opportunities for product sales and orders for products. *Systems of engagement* often overlay and complement transactional data sources, also known as *systems of record*. Geoffrey Moore has described how consumers are driving the creation of systems of engagement for collaboration and sharing and has called this a sea change for enterprise IT.[17] Figure 5-3 compares systems of record (transactions) with systems of engagement. Systems of record are structured and process-centric. Systems of engagement are unstructured and people-centric. Systems of engagement offer new opportunities for analytics. As with transactional data sources, analytics will be needed on the transactions within systems of engagement. Further, *engagement analytics*, a new type of analytics, can be used to maximize the value of systems of engagement.

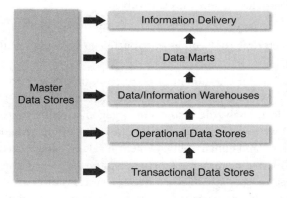

Figure 5-2   The five types of trusted data sources in IBM's information delivery architecture

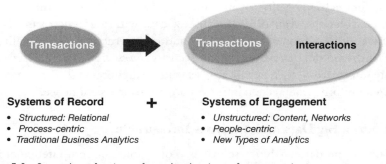

Figure 5-3   Comparison of systems of record and systems of engagement

Marie Wallace, Analytics Strategist, IBM Social Business®, has defined four engagement key performance indicators (KPIs) for systems of engagement:[18]

- **Activity:** The level of an individual's activity within a system of engagement
- **Reaction:** How others respond to an individual's activity
- **Eminence:** How others react to individuals
- **Network:** The quality of an individual's network and his or her role

Engagement analytics can be used to measure real-time engagement of a workforce or of customers. Using engagement analytics with systems of engagement can answer new questions, such as:

- How are deals closed, and who is involved?
- What characterizes interactions of successful deals?
- What characterizes the people contributing to successful deals?

When asked about the potential of systems of engagement and engagement analytics, Wallace replied, "Analyzing systems of record tells you what the company does; analyzing systems of engagement tells you how the company works. If we take this a step further, we can use engagement analytics to better understand and enhance engagement levels across a Smarter Workforce (employee), Smarter Commerce (customer), and Smarter Cities® (citizen)." Taking this yet another step further, because systems of engagement are collaborative, they offer the opportunity to embed analytics interactively using decision management, improving these systems.

Having an information agenda impacts four of the nine levers of differentiation for realizing value from data:[19] *Culture*, because an information agenda enables the availability and use of data within an enterprise; *Data*, because an information agenda directly addresses structure and formality of an organization's data governance and security; *Sponsorship*, because developing an information agenda requires executive support; and *Trust*, because having an information agenda improves organizational confidence.

Providing a Big Data and Analytics Infrastructure

While some data analytics solutions require modest computer resources and can work acceptably on a laptop computer, many data analytics solutions require a variety of software, large amounts of data storage, and significant processing resources. Building a platform of software to perform a variety of data and analytics functions can take a significant amount of time. As a supplier of IT services, the CIO can also empower groups by providing a big data and analytics infrastructure for groups to develop and run business-specific applications.

Because of the variability of resources required over time and the "bursty" nature of some analytics applications, cloud computing is an excellent delivery model for data analytics services.[20] IBM's CIO organization uses a private cloud, called Blue Insight, to provide big data and analytics services to more than 450,000 IBM users. IBM's Blue Insight cloud standardizes the data and analytics tools used by most IBM employees by delivering centralized big data and analytics services. Knowledge about the data and the business are decentralized, remaining in the business area using the cloud services. Blue Insight delivers incremental value across IBM. Value is realized through the consolidation of more than 600 data warehouses and more than 500 analytics applications.

Providing a big data and analytics infrastructure impacts two of the nine levers of differentiation for realizing value from data:[21] *Platform*, certainly, and *Sponsorship*, since an infrastructure cannot be developed without executive support.

Lessons Learned

Big data and analytics are essential to the IT function of a CIO organization. Further, the CIO is in a good position to be an important contributor to a company's big data and analytics transformation. The CIO can enable transformation of an enterprise through a wide range of activities, spanning developing big data applications to developing an information agenda to providing a big data and analytics platform to providing expertise to develop new analytics applications. Below are some of the important lessons learned.

You don't have to understand analytics technology to derive value from it. The enterprise-wide applications Faces and Watson Sales Assistant are excellent examples of users being able to use and get great value from analytics applications without needing to know how the data and analytics make them work.

Fast, cheap processors and cheap storage make analysis on big data possible. Ten years ago, a big data and analytics application such as Watson Sales Assistant, which stores and searches vast volumes of data, would have been too expensive to undertake.

It's important to leverage the levers. IBM's CIO organization is leveraging seven of the nine levers of differentiation for realizing value from data:[22] at the *Enable* level, *Source of Value* and *Platform*; at the *Drive* level, *Culture*, *Data*, and *Trust*; and at the *Amplify* level, *Sponsorship* and *Expertise*. Two levers that the CIO organization is not highly leveraging are *Funding* and *Measurement,* but this is by design, since the business units fund and measure the majority of the analytics projects.

Endnotes

1. "The Essential CIO: Insights from the Global Chief Information Officer Study," IBM Institute for Business Value, 2011. http://www-935.ibm. "com/services/c-suite/series-download.html.
2. Ibid.
3. "The Customer-Activated Enterprise: Insights from the Global C-Suite Study," IBM Institute for Business Value, 2013. http://www-935.ibm. com/services/us/en/c-suite/csuitestudy2013/.
4. Bogoleska, J., et al., "Classifying Server Behavior and Predicting Impact of Modernization Actions." The 9th International Conference on Network and Service Management, 2013. http://www.cnsm-conf.org/ 2013/documents/papers/CNSM/p59-bogojeska.pdf.
5. Balboni, F., et al., "Analytics: A Blueprint for Value—Converting Big Data and Analytics Insights into Results," IBM Institute for Business Value, 2013. http://public.dhe.ibm.com/common/ssi/ecm/en/ gbe03575usen/GBE03575USEN.PDF.
6. Schroeck, M., et al., "Analytics: The Real-World Use of Big Data: How Innovative Enterprises Extract Value from Uncertain Data," IBM Institute for Business Value, 2012. http://www-03.ibm.com/systems/ hu/resources/the_real_word_use_of_big_data.pdf.
7. Balboni, F., et al., "Analytics: A Blueprint for Value."
8. Guy, I., et al., "Best Faces Forward: A Large-Scale Study of People Search in the Enterprise," *Proceedings of the SIGCHI Conference on Human Factors in Computing Systems*, 2012. http://dl.acm.org/citation.cfm?id= 2208310.
9. Ferrucci, D., et al., "Building Watson: An Overview of the DeepQA Project," *AI Magazine*, Volume 31, Number 3, Fall 2010. http://www. aaai.org/ojs/index.php/aimagazine/article/view/2303.
10. Schroeck, M., et al., "Analytics: The Real-World Use of Big Data."
11. Balboni, F., et al., "Analytics: A Blueprint for Value."
12. Ferrucci, D., et al., "Building Watson."
13. Schroeck, M., et al., "Analytics: The Real-World Use of Big Data."
14. Balboni, F., et al., "Analytics: A Blueprint for Value."
15. Ibid.

16. Ban, L., and Marshall, A. "Connect More: Intersecting Insights from the IBM CEO, CMO and CIO Studies," IBM Institute for Business Value, 2013. http://public.dhe.ibm.com/common/ssi/ecm/en/gbe03549usen/GBE03549USEN.PDF.

17. Moore, G., "Systems of Engagement and the Future of Enterprise IT—A Sea Change in Enterprise IT," AIIM, 2011. http://www.google.com/url?sa=t&rct=j&q=&esrc=s&source=web&cd=1&cad=rja&ved=0CDQQFjAA&url=http%3A%2F%2Fwww.aiim.org%2F~%2Fmedia%2FFiles%2FAIIM%2520White%2520Papers%2FSystems-of-Engagement.pdf&ei=sPL0Uu6zGcXY0gGFzoCYDQ&usg=AFQjCNFSo9Ne5zPwcdPEYQsaceW6g5JnBg&sig2=bI-sNdgSnumdHzstwxh6PA&bvm=bv.60799247,d.cWc.

18. Wallace, M., "Maximize the Value of Your Systems of Engagement," IBM Corporation. http://www.ibm.com/engage.

19. Balboni, F., et al., "Analytics: A Blueprint for Value."

20. Yarter, L. C., "Private Cloud Delivery Model for Supplying Centralized Analytics Services," *IBM Journal of Research and Development*, Volume 56, Number 6, November/December 2012. http://ieeexplore.ieee.org/xpl/articleDetails.jsp?arnumber=6353964.

21. Balboni, F., et al., "Analytics: A Blueprint for Value."

22. Ibid.

6

Reaching Your Market

"If we can build the right digital capability that engages all the different modalities of client engagement, then we have an opportunity both to capture the data to enrich our analytics and to optimize the experience."

—Ben Edwards, Vice President, Global Communications and Digital Marketing, IBM Corporation

Perspective: Using Analytics to Reach and Engage with Clients

Within both business-to-business (B2B) and business-to-consumer (B2C) enterprises, marketing organizations are transforming themselves to become more data-centric, embracing fact-based decision making based on big data and analytics. IBM's "State of Marketing 2013" survey identified important trends in how leading companies were investing and developing marketing technology.[1] Marketing in companies is evolving and striving toward a one-to-one, or "personal marketing," approach that is supported by not just data and analytics but also automation. Developing the insights from the data and analytics approaches is not valuable unless action is taken on the analytics result. Value is driven when the insight informs a decision or drives an action. Automation enables this process and is critical to successful marketing transformations. For example, "next best action" can automate the delivery of the right offer to the right client at the right time. Chris Wong, Vice President, Strategy and Enterprise Marketing Management, views IBM's use of analytics within marketing in two distinct areas: customer analytics and performance management analytics. Both of these areas are foundational to IBM's marketing transformation.

Customer analytics include three categories of data:

- **Demographic data:** Examples are age, gender, and income.
- **Behavioral and preference data:** This data can be based on historical data and real-time data. For example, historical data for insights into how people purchased in the past and real-time data collected as they click, watch a video, or add something to a cart while online. Using both types of data, a decision can be made about making an offer in real time or via email, whichever the data indicated would be a customer's preference.
- **Time-based data:** An example is the length of time since a customer looked at a particular product or made his or her last purchase.

Performance management analytics helps determine the ROI and effectiveness of marketing actions. There are two types of performance management data:

- **Quantitative data:** Is the offer working? To what degree?
- **Qualitative data:** What other factors are impacting the offer? For example, you may find that 60% of the customers are abandoning their shopping cart because it is difficult to find the "order" button.

IBM's transformation in both customer analytics and performance management analytics is under way. Performance management analytics is further along than customer analytics, as the challenges discussed in this chapter will show. In performance management, IBM has an enterprise data warehouse with a Cognos dashboard. Because IBM historically collected customer data on companies, not individuals, the area of customer analytics is not as mature. Customer analytics represents a paradigm shift for IBM, and the individual data master project described in this chapter describes IBM's approach to this challenge.

The emphasis on personal marketing is important to both IBM and clients. Ginni Rometty's focus on marketing and the client experience was apparent in her first customer conference as CEO. This event was held in New York, where Rometty "assembled some familiar faces, the chief information officers who buy billions of dollars of software, technology services, and hardware from IBM, but she had also invited their chief marketing officers. Her ambitious—and yes, unusual—plan: Get the marketers to use IBM tools to sort their data for nuggets that will help them better reach customers and sell more stuff."[2] Clients often asked her, "What's your strategy?" Her response? "Ask me what I believe first; that's a way more enduring answer."[3]

A Signature Client Experience

Rometty believes that creating a signature client experience is what will keep IBM "essential" to clients. This signature client experience is at the heart of IBM's marketing transformation, and the use of analytics and big data are key enablers in accomplishing this goal. To underscore IBM's focus on the client experience, she created a fourth leadership team in addition to the three core teams (operating, technology, and strategy) that help guide the company. The fourth team is the Client Experience team, which she personally chairs. The members on the other teams are senior leaders in the company, while the Client Experience team members are client-facing executives. They meet monthly and bring in executives from other companies to learn from them about managing customer relationships. The goal of creating the "signature IBM relationship" is a key driver of the marketing transformation. Creating new capabilities to deliver this goal drives both IBM clients and IBM to make the investments needed.

Investments in marketing technology are expected to drive chief marketing officers (CMOs) to outspend chief information officers (CIOs) in technology purchases by 2017, according to business analyst Gartner.[4] Despite the positive trend in spending for marketing, this will not be an easy shift, either inside or outside IBM. Marketing is more accustomed to using technology "as a tool to support their creative endeavors, not the starting point."[5] Marketing's creative nature has historically lent itself to a strong belief in decisions based on "gut instinct." Insights from big data and analytics provide a different starting point for decisions and can support the creative process to improve outcomes. IDC's "Chief Marketing Officer Predictions" expected CMOs to become "masters of data" in 2013.[6] Such a transition requires a shift in the skills of the marketing organization. The predictions are that approximately half of the new hires in marketing teams are expected to come from technical backgrounds, and that is expected to grow in subsequent years as organizations realize that the skills needed in this era of marketing are shifting. The increasingly sophisticated and well-informed buyer demands a different way of interacting that CMOs will need to address. "In the wake of all of their self-education is a stream of data that the CMOs will have to understand."[7] A 2013 C-suite study by IBM's Institute for Business Value found that CMOs feel less prepared to cope with big data in 2013 than they did in 2011. For example, in 2011, 71% of CMOs felt underprepared for the data explosion; in 2013, 82% did.[8]

Marketing-Related Analytics Hiring Soaring

The availability of big data and analytics has led to a skills shortage that is impacting all industries. The skills gap gathered a lot of attention with a 2012 Harvard Business Review article titled "Data Scientist: The Sexiest Job of the 21st Century."[9] To assess just how strong the growth is for marketing organizations, Marketshare turned to icrunchdata.com for an analysis. Highlighted in *Forbes Insight*, the data showed that growth of marketing-related analytics jobs is soaring. Some sources predict that big data will create 1.9 million new jobs by 2015 in the United States alone. The growth rate in marketing-related analytics hires is noteworthy: up 67% over the past year and up 136% over the past three years.[10] This employment trend and skills gap is an area that IBM's University Relations is actively engaged in with more than 1,000 universities. Increasing analytics skills and the leadership capabilities necessary to leverage those skills is a focal point for IBM.

Agility Is Key

Ben Edwards, IBM Vice President, Global Communications and Digital Marketing, was named to BtoB's Best Marketers list in 2013 for his leadership in marketing.[11] Edwards is focused on bringing more precision and efficiency to IBM's marketing efforts. "One thing I'm particularly passionate about is adopting agile methodologies," he said. "The transformation we need to make in data-driven marketing can't be based on long cycles of execution. We have to continue to improve and create short cycles of iterative execution based on methods and outcomes."[12] One way IBM accomplishes this is through its Marketing and Communications Design Lab, which Edwards established in 2012 in New York, bringing together more than 100 dedicated people from IBM's marketing and IT groups, as well as its lead agencies. Plans are under way to expand the program through a global network of Marketing and Communications Design Labs (M&C Labs). "M&C Lab is the intersection point for how we engage with our agency partners and partners in our own IT organization to deliver marketing outcomes," Edwards said.

The use of analytics in marketing has expanded beyond measuring effectiveness. Big data and social media analytics are game-changing technologies that enable forward-thinking marketing organizations to engage with clients in new ways and on entirely new levels. Making sense of the oceans of data and using it to create the signature client experience needed to differentiate in the marketplace will take skills and determination. The challenges are many, and the following real-world examples cover some of the many marketing initiatives under way at IBM.

Challenge: Developing the Data Foundation and Analytics Capability to Enable a Signature Client Experience

Chris Wong, IBM Vice President, Strategy and Product Management, refers to the current era of buyers being better informed than in the past as the "golden age of marketing." Why would this be the golden age of marketing? This is the era when buyers have access to a wealth of resources and come to the buying process "smarter" than ever before. Some view this as a challenge or threat to their existing business model, but if you believe a central goal of marketing is to understand customers, respond to their needs, and understand how best to engage with them, then big data and analytics can enable that capability in ways that were not possible before. There are significant challenges in this era, but the opportunities it creates are unprecedented. To address these challenges and seize the opportunities in marketing, IBM has several analytics initiatives under way.

Marketing at IBM has two concurrent approaches for leveraging big data and analytics in process:

- **Transactional analytics:** Transactional analytics is performance based and helps leaders understand the effectiveness of various marketing actions. For example, web analytics provides insights into the effectiveness of an offer through tracking of click-throughs.
- **Behavioral analytics:** This is a more sophisticated set of analytics from a marketing perspective. Wong refers to this approach as the "Holy Grail" for analytics in marketing, whether it is for a B2C or a B2B company. Behavioral analytics provides insights into the decision processes of individual people making purchasing decisions. B2C enterprises have been using behavioral analytics to improve business outcomes for some time,

yet applying these techniques in a B2B enterprise is different. Wong observed that many of IBM's early forays into analytics have been to drive insights from the transactional and performance-based analytics. While these are considered descriptive analytics, understanding the current state provides a solid foundation for then predicting future outcomes. For example, performance analytics is used to determine whether the pipeline of sales leads is meeting targets, and then a prediction based on expected win rates can indicate what corrective action will need to be taken. The problem can be identified using this approach, but further analytics modeling is needed to determine the root cause and what corrective action can be taken. The IBM Marketing organization is working on the analytics approaches to discover root causes and recommended corrective actions and that input will be used in the development of simulation models. Models need to be refreshed as the market or product life cycle evolution changes to ensure that predictions and corrective actions continue to be effective.

One of the significant challenges for a B2B enterprise wanting to leverage behavioral analytics is that the underlying legacy data is collected not at the individual decision maker level, but instead at an enterprise level. IBM's data historically has been transactional systems of records based on companies and is limited in terms of the behavioral analytics that can be applied. Behavioral analytics requires the data to be captured at the individual level to provide a customized, relevant client experience. B2C companies, particularly those that started with online business models, have collected data at the individual level for some time, and the leaders are leveraging analytics to drive sales very effectively. So, how does IBM build on the vast legacy enterprise transactional data collected to understand individual business purchase behaviors and deliver signature client experiences?

A major initiative was launched to address this question with the CIO's office to build the individual data master project. This new data capability at IBM will capture and instrument every individual's interaction with IBM in order to provide a relevant signature experience. This ambitious initiative is omni-channel in scope, with the intent of understanding client preferences through data collected on the website (for example, which offerings were explored), events (for example, which conferences or briefings were attended), interactions with sales, support desk interactions, and so on. Omni-channel in this instance refers to the customer unified view of a brand while multi-channel is the operational side of processes and strategies within the channels. The intent is to capture preferences and interests at the individual level from each interaction with the company and provide a customized experience based on those preferences. Given the scale—with IBM operating in more than 170 countries and the many channels of interaction—this is a significant undertaking.

With the individual data master records, IBM will be able to use predictive analytics to help clients through their buying journey, which Wong refers to as the "learn, solve, compare, and purchase" process. Understanding the types of information or interactions that the individual could use before even talking to a sales representative would provide a better client experience and business outcome. Predictive analytics will be leveraged to determine the right offer for the individual at a particular phase in the process. Many retailers have made strides to get the right offer to the right customer at the right time through mobile apps that detect when a customer is in a store, know the person's preferences, and then text an offer based on that profile. For IBM, this initiative is a large, multi-year effort. While an online retailer would only need to instrument its website to capture this data, or a brick-and-mortar retailer to instrument its store and website, IBM needs to instrument its website, marketing and sales events, marketing automation system, sales and support channels experiences, and more to develop a holistic view of how to best interact with the client and provide the signature experience at each of those touch points. The challenge for IBM is moving from enterprise data to focusing on buying decision makers and instrumenting the process. While this work is under way, a key underpinning is the marketing automation system, which will link with the web system and the customer relationship marketing (CRM) system around the individual client.

Outcome: Individual Data Master to Provide Client-Level Insights

The challenge to instrument and collect data at the client level in a B2B environment on the scale IBM is undertaking is significant. The work is in progress and will continue, with new capabilities being added iteratively as the teams work on the marketing transformation.

Challenge: Providing a Real-Time View into Effectiveness of Marketing Actions: Performance Management

The business challenge was to track the performance of offer metrics and set the foundation for end-to-end predictive capabilities. Melody Dunn, Director, Marketing Systems, Corporate M&C, has been involved in driving this marketing transformation. In 2009, the **IBM Enterprise Marketing Management (EMM) Automation Project** began, and by 2011, the team had deployed this system to the local marketing teams in 79 countries in 18 months. Four modules were deployed simultaneously: EMM Campaign, EMM Collaboration (in later versions called EMM Distributed Marketing), EMM eMessage, and EMM Leads. With Cognos, the Marketing organization added capabilities to do real-time reporting around open rates, click-through rates, bounce-backs, number of emails sent, and how many offers were downloaded. Offer statistics were available in real time with the 2012 EMM Operations Offer Management capability. All offers were classified and tracked through the system, enabling a feedback process on what is working or not in real time. In addition, metrics were available on validated lead revenue and win revenue.

While this work was under way, the back-end infrastructure project was happening simultaneously to collect the data. Key metrics were defined and instrumented to enable predictive and prescriptive analytics. The goal to provide an "early warning system" is similar to the goal of providing an early warning system for quality problems described in Chapter 3, "Optimizing the Supply Chain." For example, if the industry benchmark for email open rates is 17% for similar types of business, and if IBM is less than that, a warning to take action would be issued. The solution is being built to provide the warning as well as possible causes (audience may have been too large, criteria for offer may have been wrong, timing was bad, etc.) so that corrective actions can be taken. With instrumentation on other key noise metrics, earlier triggers and warnings will be enabled.

Propensity-to-buy models are leveraged heavily internally at the company and brand levels. These models will evolve continuously as the individual data master discussed in the previous section will enable additional capabilities. The propensity-to-buy models will not only predict when and what a client may be interested in but their behaviors as well (such as who their key influencers are and what information they needed for a decision).

Outcome: Marketing Efficiencies Realized and Transformation of Marketing Enabled

Many outcomes are derived from linking the IBM EMM automation system with other technologies to automate demand generation and campaign management within IBM. For example, "IBM has streamlined its content syndication process, which previously required 30 days to create response handling and landing page URLs. Using a web-based registration page creation tool developed by IBM, demand programs professionals can register the tactic into IBM EMM in two hours or less. Through the automated solution, loading of responses now takes one day instead of a week, and follow-up time for transactional emails has been cut from a week to an hour."[13] Figure 6-1 highlights some of the additional outcomes.

IBM climbed to the #3 spot on Interbrand's Best Global Brands, no small accomplishment for a B2B enterprise in a list dominated by consumer brands.

The Science
Applied automation and analytics for smarter demand generation. Partnering with the CIO team, IBM marketing moved from a "spray and pray" marketing approach that took some 7M emails to deliver a message to prospective clients to just over 500,000 emails using automated marketing.

7M

500,000

The result: a response rate 14x greater with the new approach. In one major market, lead conversion has doubled.

The Discipline
Created IBM's Program Framework to align marketing investments to client needs, instead of IBM products. In year one, consolidated 80+ marketing programs into 12.

Created Global Centers of Excellence for marketing operations and market insights to improve performance and productivity.

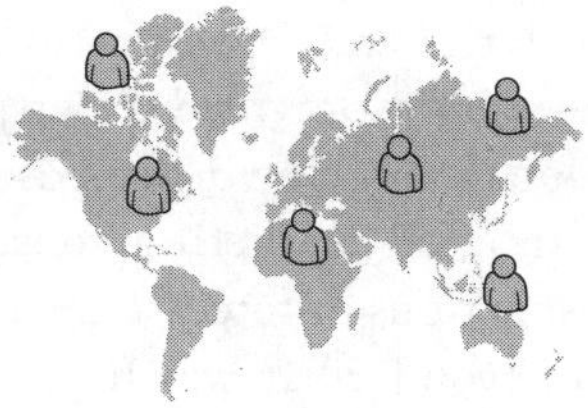

Source: "Creating a Smarter Enterprise—The Science of Transformation," IBM. http://public.dhe.ibm.com/common/ssi/ecm/en/gbe03584usen/GBE03584USEN.PDF.

Figure 6-1 IBM marketing automation and analytics initiatives drive efficiencies

As the capabilities from both the infrastructure and marketing automation project combine, one anticipated business value is a shift in behavior within the Marketing organization. Historically, many marketers measured success in terms of volume of execution—for example, measuring success based on how many emails were sent or how many events held rather than the outcomes from the actions. With big data and analytics and the individual data master, targeted offers and signature client experiences will be the focus. More offers, more tactics, more touches are counterproductive in this golden era, in which analytics capabilities enable marketing to provide a signature client experience.

As mentioned earlier, another significant impact resulting from big data and analytics is that the skills needed in marketing organizations have shifted. More data scientists and leaders who can leverage evidence-based decision processes are in demand. Historically, the majority of the marketing skills were in project management, managing work with agencies, brands, etc. Demands for analytics skills in marketing is expected to remain very high as companies compete for the scarce talent. Dunn sums it up well: "Our job is to be the marketing transformation leaders who are the custodians of the future vision and to understand how marketing technology can enable that vision to come true."

Challenge: Going Beyond Correlation to Determine Causal Effects of Marketing Actions

The 2010 article "Analyzing Causal Effects with Observational Studies for Evidence-Based Marketing at IBM" recommended a methodology to apply science to marketing decisions through the use of observational studies in order to develop an understanding of the cause-and-effect relationships between treatments and outcomes.[14] Stefanos Manganaris, Manager, Business Analytics and Optimization, IBM Inside Sales, was a co-author on this article, which provided a perspective on how marketing could drive business value through evidence-based marketing.

Internal marketing consulting at IBM aimed to "elucidate the effects of past actions or forecast the effects of planned actions."[15] The challenge was to go beyond what was happening (correlation) and to understand true causal effects of marketing actions. Two case studies from the paper demonstrate the use of observational studies to better inform marketing decisions at IBM. The first case study involves an analysis of the role special contract terms and conditions had on follow-on revenue for a particular hardware system. The hypothesis was that "special terms allowed the client to more easily and affordably make such follow-on purchase from IBM."[16] Historical data was used, and 3,300 eligible contracts for 1,200 clients in the United States over a six-year period were examined. Of those, 42% have the special terms and conditions. The key measured outcome was revenue from follow-on business over a three-year period once the contract was signed.

Outcome: System Deals with Special Terms and Conditions Added Grew from 67% to 98% over Three Quarters

The findings from the study were used to motivate the sales force for the hardware system to include the special terms and conditions in their deals. Marketing actions were also launched to promote such deals, and the incentive sales plan was modified to encourage inclusion of these terms and conditions. The observational study and evidence-backed insights convinced senior leaders to take steps to include the terms and conditions in certain types of these system deals. It was estimated that for each percentage point of broader adoption, the terms drove about $10 million of new revenue annually. Further evidence of the adoption of the findings is that the proportion of these system deals increased from 67% in fourth quarter 2007 to 89% in first quarter 2008 and to 98% in second quarter 2008 (see Figure 6-2). This project won a prestigious internal award, Market Development & Insights Innovation Award, in 2008.

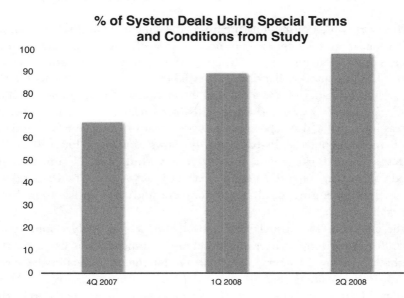

% of System Deals Using Special Terms and Conditions from Study

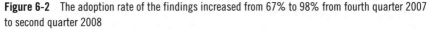

Figure 6-2 The adoption rate of the findings increased from 67% to 98% from fourth quarter 2007 to second quarter 2008

A second example of applying this methodology was a market basket analysis. This case looked at the likelihood of increasing the odds to win in deals that combined a hardware system with a services offering. The hypothesis was that IBM had higher odds of winning the system deal when the leads were pursued in collaboration with services—offering a more complete solution to the client. The executive sponsor had a gut feeling that the win rates would improve but wanted evidence to convince the two distinct silos to work together. Several important questions needed to be answered: Did the benefits of collaboration outweigh the possible drawbacks (e.g., from increasing the complexity of the deal)? If collaboration were to be actively promoted, would the partnership truly be a win–win proposition? What would be the value of the collaboration for each partner?

Approximately 50,000 leads for 16,000 clients in the United States over a three-year period were examined. Each of these examples used a sensitivity analysis to understand how the conclusion could change if there were an unobserved difference. The study confirmed that this go-to-market approach was a win–win proposition for the system and services teams.

Challenge: Tapping into Analytics Passion to Provide New Insights to Inform IBM's Digital Strategy

This story, which varies in nature from others included in this book, showcases a fun, innovative approach to driving an analytics culture and gaining business insights along the way. In 2012, IBM held the first "Crunch Day." Crunch Day was an idea that came to Keith Hermiz, Research Scientist, IBM Research, and leader of the Analytics Practitioners Community in IBM, while watching *Iron Chef* and other skills-based reality shows on television. He was intrigued and saw potential to utilize many of the same key ingredients found in popular skills-based reality shows as a recipe for stimulating interest in applying big data and analytics within IBM. Hermiz's recipe called for mixing talented people, extraordinary circumstances, and an extremely challenging deadline to compete and accomplish something remarkable.

The challenge for Crunch Day participants was to analyze more than 400,000 tweets from Twitter and develop recommendations based on the insights all within 24 hours. The challenge for the organizers of the event was to find a business sponsor who would be willing to use the insights developed from Crunch Day. The Marketing organization stepped up to the challenge, and Edwards became the business sponsor of the event.

Each team had to sift through the unstructured data to produce insights and recommendations that could be distilled into an executive summary. The teams presented their findings, in 10-minute increments, to a panel of eight judges, including senior executives.

The insights from the Crunch Day teams have impacted IBM's digital strategy and development efforts since 2012, helping guide the IBM brands and press teams' work on various social channels. The 130 volunteer participants spanned the globe and came together across 12 time zones to form 14 teams. The event was held again in 2013, with a focus on social business adoption, and has become an annual tradition.

"Crunch Day was a really exciting experience for me and the team....The business issue that the business sponsor was interested in learning about was how IBM's presence on Twitter is impacting messages around various key topics such as Big Data, IBM PureSystems® and the Master's Golf tournament," said Hardik Dave, IBM Senior Business Analyst.

Outcome: Insights from Diverse Teams Provided the Evidence Needed to Make Changes to the Digital Strategy

The Crunch Day event yielded several key findings. One finding was that IBM has a significant voice in the discussion on IBM-related topics on Twitter both through IBM's official Twitter IDs and those of individual IBM employees. This can be taken as positive or negative and has to be carefully planned by the marketing and communication teams. Crunch Day provided proof points that significantly influenced IBM's social strategy. One insight was that IBM wasn't listening as effectively as thought via social media, and corrective actions were taken. Another important finding was that a competitor was being more effective on key performance indicators that are important to IBM; IBM took action and provided funding to address the issue. This led IBM to take a series of actions, including a shift in marketing investment, to ensure that IBM's message was more focused and effective in that channel. The business sponsor, Edwards, remarked, "One of the great things about working at IBM is the vast pool of talented people you can tap into. Crunch Day is a perfect example. I was impressed by the insights the IBM analysts community extracted from the Twitter data. They offered us a powerful view about how our brand is experienced on Twitter—and some great ideas for how to improve the signal-to-noise ratio."

Ross Mauri, IBM Vice President, Analytics and Social Transformation (and a Crunch Day judge), commented, "I was very impressed by the diversity of the insights from across the teams, the creativity of the approaches taken, and the variety of tools used in the global collaborations."

The reality show aspect of this event was that 14 teams came together quickly to analyze the same data set and to develop a wide array of insights that influenced the business. Doug Dow, Vice President, Business Analytics Transformation, and Brenda Dietrich, IBM Fellow and Vice President, Emerging Technologies, IBM Watson, co-sponsored the event. Dow observed, "Crunch Day showcased how analytics can help make IBM smarter in an innovative way."

Dietrich said, "I was pleased to see the level of participation and diversity of teams, how people came together to analyze a high-volume, low-signal data set; there was a lot of irrelevant data, and the teams distilled which elements had value for a real business end user."

Lessons Learned

Don't boil the data ocean. While the Marketing organization is working on developing the client-level data that was historically not collected, it is not waiting for "perfect data" to drive value from analytics now. Each project works with the data available and uses agile development to incorporate new capabilities and data sources as they become available.

It's important to leverage the levers. The Marketing organization is enabling the use of big data and analytics through the use of the three foundational levers *Source of Value, Measurement,* and *Platform* outlined in "Analytics: A Blueprint for Value" and discussed in Chapter 1, "Why Big Data and Analytics?" Through the executive leadership, the Marketing organization has demonstrated the use of the *Sponsorship* lever; by taking the innovative step to be the first business sponsor of Crunch Day, the Marketing organization has worked the *Culture* lever to change the decision-making process.

Relationships inferred from data today may not be present in data collected tomorrow. The example of the methodology that can be used in marketing to determine causal events will help drive a deeper understanding of the insights from the data. The relationships inferred may change quickly, necessitating an agile development environment to ensure that the inferences stay current. Does this mean that the analysis is not worth doing if it can change so quickly? No, but it does mean that using an agile development environment that can quickly respond to changes will be most advantageous.

Analytics projects can be short and fun and can have a big impact. When Crunch Day was first conceived, the objective was to get more people interested in analytics and to have some fun in the process. It was designed to raise awareness about analytics, connect analytics practitioners and novices alike who were interested in it, and help drive the widespread use of analytics across the company. Producing valuable business insights in 24 hours was not a critical success factor for Crunch Day, but when that happened, it showed just how powerful even short, fun analytics projects or events can be.

Endnotes

1. "The State of Marketing 2013, IBM's Global Survey of Marketers," IBM, 2013. http://www-01.ibm.com/software/marketing-solutions/campaigns/surveys/2013-marketers-survey.html.
2. "IBM's Ginni Rometty Looks Ahead," *CNN Money,* September 2012. http://management.fortune.cnn.com/2012/09/20/powerful-women-rometty-ibm/.

3. "Transcript: IBM's Ginni Rometty on Leadership," *CNN Money*, October 2012. http://management.fortune.cnn.com/2012/10/02/transcript-ibms-ginni-rometty-on-leadership/.

4. "Big Data: CMO Set to Outspend CIO on Data-Crunching Technology," *Marketing*, August 2012. http://www.marketingmag.com.au/news/big-data-cmo-set-to-outspend-cio-on-data-crunching-technology-17274/#.UsNfL3dcVb2.

5. "IBM's Ginni Rometty Looks Ahead."

6. "Trend Report: CMOs and CIOs Will End 2013 as Either Friend or 'Frenemy,'" *Marketing*, January 2013. http://www.marketingmag.com.au/news/trend-report-cmos-and-cios-will-end-2013-as-either-friend-or-frenemy-33922/#.UsNhJndcVb2.

7. Ibid.

8. "The Customer-Activated Enterprise—Insights from the C-Suite Global Study," IBM Institute for Business Value, 2013. http://www-01.ibm.com/common/ssi/cgi-bin/ssialias?subtype=XB&infotype=PM&appname=GBSE_GB_TI_USEN&htmlfid=GBE03572USEN&attachment=GBE03572USEN.PDF.

9. Davenport, T. H., and Patil, D. J., "Data Scientist: The Sexiest Job of the 21st Century." *Harvard Business Review*, October 2012. http://hbr.org/2012/10/data-scientist-the-sexiest-job-of-the-21st-century/.

10. Kehrer, D., "Analysis Shows Jump in Marketing Analytics Jobs," *Forbes Insight*, August 2013. http://www.forbes.com/sites/forbesinsights/2013/08/02/analysis-shows-jump-in-marketing-analytics-jobs/.

11. BtoBs 2013 Best. http://edit.btobonline.com/section/best2013.

12. Maddox, K., "BtoB's Best Marketers—Ben Edwards, IBM Corp. VP-Global Communications and Digital Marketing," *Advertising Age*, October 2013. http://adage.com/article/btob/btob-s-marketers-ben-edwards-ibm-corp/290418/.

13. "IBM Seeing Internal Payoffs from Marketing Automation with Unica Integration." *The Future of Digital Engagement*, May 2011. http://www.demandgenreport.com/industry-topics/revenue-strategies/1580-ibm-seeing-internal-payoffs-from-marketing-automation-with-unica-integration-.html#.UsB01HdcVb0.

14. Manganaris, S., et al., "Analyzing Causal Effects with Observational Studies for Evidence-Based Marketing at IBM," *The Berkeley Electronic Press*, Volume 8, 2010.

15. Ibid.

16. Ibid.

7

Measuring the Immeasurable

"If you are not challenging the status quo with your analytics project, you are not driving transformation."

—Nick Kadochnikov, Executive Program Manager, Business Analytics Transformation, IBM Corporation

Perspective: Software Development Organization Optimizes the Highly Skilled Workforce

Investments totaling more than $17 billion in 34 analytics software acquisitions between 2005 and 2013 are proof that this market matters to IBM. The acquisitions have not only shifted IBM's product portfolio, they have changed the skill mix and culture of IBM's employees and leaders. For example, two executives from acquisitions are now driving a transformation of IBM's product development. Doug Dow from the SPSS acquisition and Jean-François Abramatic from the ILOG® acquisition initially worked within IBM's Software division, integrating their respective companies into IBM. They have since moved into key transformation roles, addressing issues far beyond the scope of the ILOG and SPSS brands. Abramatic took the position of Director, Development Productivity and Innovation, in the newly established Development Enterprise Transformation Initiative, while Dow became Vice President, Business Analytics Transformation. Both of these roles were newly created positions with broad mandates to drive business outcomes through analytics. Abramatic and Dow had known each other while at ILOG and SPSS, respectively, so when they moved into their transformation roles, it was natural for them to collaborate and seek advice from each other.

IBM has long used analytics in its supply chain and has made great progress applying analytics in finance, workforce management, and several other parts of the enterprise. However, in 2011, there were no visible analytics projects under way for the software development organizations. Together Dow and Abramatic created a proposal to use analytics to transform how and where IBM product developers work. Figure 7-1 shows the global software lab locations. Abramatic partnered with Dow and one of Dow's project leaders, Nick Kadochnikov, to measure what many considered impossible to measure due to the significant data challenges and complexity and scale. The project was necessary because, as the old adage says, "you can't manage what you can't measure," and this had prevented effective use of analytics in IBM's software product development for many years.

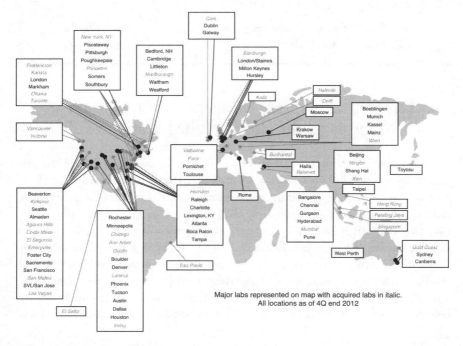

Figure 7-1   Global software lab locations

Challenge: Creating a Common View of Development Expense to Enable Decision Making

The business challenge was to create a common, holistic view of the development expense across products and geographies in order to make more fact-based decisions about resources. Hardware and software developers are located around the globe, yet there was no common expense or productivity view of this critical resource. Having a set of common metrics and profiles for the development organizations would enable those resources to be measured more effectively so they could establish "best of breed" practices, gain efficiencies, and drive further improvements. With a global team, it is important to be able to understand developer productivity as a function of team composition along multiple dimensions, such as geography, position, and experience; to understand the impact of distributed development; and to evaluate future development workforce plans under various economic scenarios. This project laid a foundation for accomplishing these objectives.

Development Expense Baseline Project

When considering options for leveraging analytics within the software development organization, it became clear that a foundational project—which came to be called the **Development Expense Baseline Project**—was an essential first step. This foundational project would enable many other uses of analytics, and without it, many other projects would not be possible. Because it was an *enabling* project rather than one that could demonstrate an immediate ROI on its own, building the business case was challenging. The foundational project was competing for funding against more well-defined, but less far-reaching, projects. The baseline project involved breaking down both silos of authority *and* silos of data. Data from Human Resources, Finance, and many other functions was needed to develop a consistent and holistic baseline view of development expense that could be used to measure the total business impact of changes in development processes. In fact, when Kadochnikov conducted early subject matter expert interviews, the most common feedback he received was "that is impossible to do." A particularly revealing response was "If I was given this as a project to do, I would find another job!" Fortunately, Kadochnikov likes a challenge, and hearing that this task was "impossible" motivated him to think of innovative ways to "do the impossible."

Analytics projects frequently break down data barriers by aggregating data that is originally housed across multiple systems. As analytics becomes widely deployed within the functional units of an organization, expanding the use of analytics often requires also breaking down organizational barriers, which can be far more difficult. Human Resources (HR) organizations naturally protect data about employees, so when requests were made to access this data for the project, IBM HR's initial response was, not surprisingly, negative. The Finance organization had an equally protective wall around the expense and revenue data that Abramatic and Kadochnikov needed. While there were many hurdles to overcome to get the right data to build the foundation, the compelling part of this story is that the analytics team knew it would take years and a lot of funding to collect the right data. So instead of waiting, they chose to leverage analytics to compensate for the imperfect and incomplete data that was immediately available to them (see Figure 7-2).

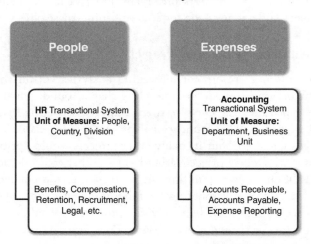

Information Contained in Two Separate Transactional Systems

People

HR Transactional System
Unit of Measure: People, Country, Division

Benefits, Compensation, Retention, Recruitment, Legal, etc.

Expenses

Accounting Transactional System
Unit of Measure: Department, Business Unit

Accounts Receivable, Accounts Payable, Expense Reporting

Figure 7-2 Analytics project requiring silos of data needs to align HR-derived information about what people do with where company incurs development expenses

The baseline project is designed to help optimize the workforce, a goal that many enterprises share. IBM has many software products grouped into what IBM refers to as "brands," with each brand having its own development team. As IBM moved from being a multinational corporation to a globally integrated enterprise, several organizational changes were put in place to enable transformation. The concept of the globally integrated enterprise was outlined in an article by former IBM CEO Sam Palmisano and published by the Council on Foreign Relations in 2006:

> Businesses are changing in fundamental ways—structurally, operationally, and culturally—in response to the imperatives of globalization and new technology. As CEO and chair of the board of IBM, I have observed this within IBM and among our clients. And I believe that rather than continuing to focus on past models, regulators, scholars, nongovernmental organizations, community leaders, and business executives would be best served by thinking about the global corporation of the future and its implications for new approaches.[1]

The globally integrated enterprise structure that Palmisano described enabled functions like the development organization to create a holistic capability across the organization as opposed to operating within vertical silos.

The globally integrated enterprise business model is "the real story behind IBM's success in the course Palmisano set for 21st century global enterprises. Recognizing that the company's command-and-control culture wouldn't work in the 21st century, he defined leadership as leading by values and created a unique collaborative organizational structure," observed Bill George in the Bloomberg blog entry "How IBM's Sam Palmisano Redefined the Global Corporation."[2] The Development Enterprise Transformation Initiative (Dev ETI) is an organizational structure that was created following this redefinition. It was designed to help all of the development functions across IBM transform by improving the effectiveness and efficiency of their development processes.

Abramatic and the team knew that they would need to work with each development organization in order to gain acceptance and adoption of new tools and processes. Driving change, especially change involving tools and processes, is often a significant challenge. Development organizations are not easily convinced that new processes or tools will provide benefit. Phase one of the Development Expense Baseline Project was designed to create a common understanding and acceptance of IBM spending for each development function across multiple brands, organizations, and countries. Once phase one established that common understanding, the second phase of the project, the Development Productivity Indicators Project, which measures productivity across development functions, is being developed in close alliance with the project stakeholders—members of multiple development teams. Iterative and agile implementation of analytics solutions with extensive new user involvement and feedback is critical to the success and adoption of the project. The project's goal was to create models that could be used to better understand the operation of IBM's development organizations. Iterative joint implementation of analytics tools, involving both the business user and the analytics practitioner, improves the correctness and, more importantly, the usefulness of the models used within the analytics tools.

Abramatic credits IBM's organizational focus on transformation and the existence of groups, such as his and Dow's, whose mission is to drive transformation, with enabling this powerful foundational work. While no single brand would be likely to take on an "impossible" but necessary task, an organization whose mission is transformation provides the structure and culture to challenge assumptions, break barriers, and make the business case for change. While the term *foundational* seems apt, this foundation could not have been put in without groundbreaking insights that enabled the team to see what was possible and overcome the obstacles that were in the way.

The Development Expense Baseline Project journey had three significant challenges:

- Data
- Tools and infrastructure
- Organization

The project followed a tried-and-true recipe for analytics success: pairing the domain subject matter expertise with analytics know-how. While Kadochnikov led implementation of the analytics tools, Peter Bradford, a member of the Dev ETI team, provided domain expertise, guidance, and personal connections to the development organizations.

The data challenge had several aspects:

- Gaining access to data was difficult.
- Once accessed, the data was difficult to work with.
- The data contained "noise."
- The data existed in many different silos.
- Much of the data was not regularly maintained.

Kadochnikov spent a significant amount of this time on data challenges. He had to take approximately 60 steps just to normalize the data fields so that data from different sources could be correctly combined and compared.

The data challenges mostly stemmed from the fact that the existing data marts, such as finance, accounting, and HR, were not designed to support consistently measuring the spending associated with each development function across the Development teams. Consistency of the measurement was critically important to enable benchmarking and sharing of best practices.

This was, however, difficult to achieve, given that the Software group included several recent acquisitions, and the Development workforce was distributed around the globe. Inconsistencies were very significant. For example, job titles did not mean the same thing in different development organizations and were often not descriptive of the work being done by the developers. This is not surprising, given that this information resulted from multiple acquisitions and had to comply with country-specific rules. The information originally had very different purposes—namely, to retain and compensate the talent—both of which are primary HR functions.

The team fed all available job type–related variables into the model. HR established each of the variables for a different purpose, but combining all of them together provided great value in leveraging a multivariate approach to create "best of breed" information within as well as across the variables. System variables from legacy sources, such as organization name, ID, primary job role, job category, position, and job code, were combined with employee self-provided information such as job description from the internal Blue Pages (IBM's enterprise staff directory).

Once all the information was combined, the team derived a series of business rules. The team learned, for example, that an individual with the title Application Developer in one organization might do a very different job than the person with the same primary job role in another organization. Self-provided job description information from Blue Pages was extremely helpful. However, Blue Pages couldn't be used on its own due to hundreds of variations of how the same job could be described by employees. Once a consistent classification structure was established, mapped, and validated with multiple stakeholders, the team had a common view of the Development resources and what they were working on. That was just the first step in the quest to create an enterprise-level view of development expense.

IBM's financial and accounting systems do not track revenue and expense data at the individual employee level. Generally speaking, expenses are available at the department level and above. On top of that, the way the department codes are captured in financial systems and HR systems varies. There are multiple special accounting rules for most of the development organizations, representing how the research and development labs are funded by the project sponsors or parent organizations.

Dealing with these special accounting rules was time-consuming and required intimate knowledge of the underlying data. The team had to derive hundreds of heuristic rules based on manual reviews of thousands of data records and by learning the intricacies of how development expenses were allocated for each laboratory or research project. The manual review exercise unveiled several surprises. For example, there was no research expense for Switzerland, while according to the HR data, the project team could see a large development laboratory located in Zurich. Each of these special rules had to be understood and resolved in order for the project to succeed. The team learned why the experts who were consulted early on said this was an impossible task.

While the analytics objective was to allocate the expense to each development employee role to enable further aggregation, the team also had to ensure that the accounting totals were kept intact so that the business executives and finance staff could recognize overall aggregated expense figures. Given that traditional modeling techniques could not handle this type of aggregated data and the differences in departments, divisions, and even country designators, the analytics team had to take a rather unconventional approach.

This approach involved the use of text mining; the team extracted, for example, heuristic concepts from job descriptions and generated approximately 890 rules to apply to one cross-IBM job taxonomy. Once the job assignments were determined, a training set of expense data and a lowest-level common denominator between the two separate sources of data was created. Given the variations in designation of department between accounting systems and HR, as well as special accounting rules, allocating actual department spending to each employee was not possible. And given the aggregated nature of the accounting data, traditional modeling techniques for missing variable imputation didn't produce acceptable results. After multiple attempts, the project team found a successful combination by using the "nearest neighbor" algorithm to predict expense for employees "like the employees with known expense." The team then leveraged iterative proportional fitting, a technique frequently deployed by organizations like the U.S. Census Bureau, to ensure that overall accounting totals aligned with accounting records.

The production version of the Development Expense Baseline Project was built using a combination of IBM SPSS Modeler, which was used for text mining and classification, and IBM SPSS Statistics, which was used for data preparation, transformation, and deployment of the nearest neighbor and iterative proportional fitting models. In total, there were approximately 900 text analytics rules and more than 4,000 lines of code in IBM SPSS Statistics to enable a push-button process that outputs a consistent expense for each type of development activity across 43,000 employees.

Everyone on the team understands just how important it is to earn the trust of those who will use the Development Expense Baseline Project. Bradford and Kadochnikov spent significant time with the stakeholders and members of development teams to discuss the use cases, share the model, confirm the logic, and explore how the project can be employed across IBM development organizations. A cooperative, collaborative approach is being used to reach the best outcome. More challenges are ahead as the Development ETI team works to get this analytics model adopted and deployed across the company's software development organizations.

Outcome: Development Expense Baseline Project Proves That the Immeasurable Can Be Measured

The important take-away from this experience is that the team was able to use analytics to do what was considered impossible. The team made it possible to view expense at a level of granularity that had previously not been available. With that additional level of granularity came business insights needed to drive actions. But the team did not just do the cross-matching to get to that level of detail and then run with it. They took the time to cross-match the information, to validate it at a very granular level, and to build the trust needed in the data for people to make decisions based on it.

This project tackled an area previously thought to be impossible, and in the years ahead, it will make possible other projects that could not have previously been considered.

Lessons Learned

Analytics can be used to fill gaps in imperfect data. With the Development Expense Baseline project, the data challenges were significant, and the team had to come up with approaches to fill in gaps to accomplish the goal. Analytics provided a way to fill those data gaps and reconcile disparate data and definitions across the many silos of information.

Investing in a foundation project will enable new opportunities in the future. Leadership and commitment investment made this foundational project possible, and future value will be driven as other analytics projects build from it.

It's important to leverage the levers. As covered in Chapter 1, "Why Big Data and Analytics?" organizations that excel in leveraging the nine levers of differentiation derive the most value from big data and analytics.[3] The

Development Expense Baseline Project worked the *Source of Value* lever through creating a new holistic view of development expense. It also used the *Measurement* lever through the innovative creation of a capability to measure what had previously been too complex to measure. It also used the *Data* lever through a concerted effort to engage with and validate the model in order to build the confidence needed in the data for people to make decisions based on it.

Endnotes

1. Palmisano, S. J., "The Globally Integrated Enterprise," *Foreign Affairs*, May/June 2006. http://www.foreignaffairs.com/articles/61713/samuel-j-palmisano/the-globally-integrated-enterprise.
2. George, B., "How IBM's Sam Palmisano Redefined the Global Corporation," *Bloomberg*, January 20, 2012. http://www.bloomberg.com/news/2012-01-20/how-ibm-s-sam-palmisano-redefined-the-global-corporation.html.
3. Balboni, F., et al., "Analytics: A Blueprint for Value—Converting Big Data and Analytics into Results," IBM Institute for Business Value, November 2013. http://public.dhe.ibm.com/common/ssi/ecm/en/gbe03575usen/GBE03575USEN.PDF.

8

Optimizing Manufacturing

"The application of advanced analytics to the massive data associated with semiconductor manufacturing has driven significant improvements in both product quality control and productivity. Perhaps more significantly, over the long term, such analyses have enabled the discovery of previously unknown mechanisms influencing product performance."

–Robert J. Baseman, Senior Technical Scientist, IBM Research, IBM Corporation ·

Perspective: Applying Analytics to Manufacturing and Product Management

IBM faces challenges similar to most other manufacturers, including manufacturers of electronics, automobiles, and consumer packaged goods. Manufacturers strive to be highly efficient, manage costs and resources, forecast supply and demand, and more. Manufacturing processes, both within IBM and in other enterprises, benefit significantly from the use of analytics to improve outcomes. For example, manufacturing equipment can be instrumented with sensors that enable early warnings and a predictive maintenance application. Data from sensors and transactional data stores stream in at increasing rates, and manufacturers can use analytics to gain insights and improve outcomes.

IBM has been using techniques that are now called *analytics* in its semiconductor design, development, and manufacturing since at least the late 1950s. Collecting data about semiconductor devices and analyzing the statistical properties of that data has been a routine part of the development and manufacturing of semiconductors for decades. For example, during manufacturing of a silicon device, the device is subjected to a number of electrical tests to determine whether it is performing according to the target specification. Data is collected during the manufacturing of semiconductors and analyzed to determine changes in the manufacturing process that will improve the product yield (the portion of the devices that perform correctly). Optimization techniques have been used for decades in the manufacturing of semiconductors, circuit cards, and other computer components for problems ranging from manufacturing line layout to production scheduling. For example, in 1960, IBM used linear programming to determine production schedules for its manufacturing lines. The use of analytics in semiconductor design and manufacturing has advanced greatly since the 1960s, as increased computing speed and improved mathematical algorithms have dramatically increased the size of problems that can be routinely solved.

Of the many stories that could have been selected for this chapter, three were selected from IBM's state-of-the-art, data-rich 300-millimeter semiconductor fabrication plant:

- One story is about the complex optimization scheduler for planning work on the manufacturing line.
- Another story is about using big data and analytics to increase the yield in the manufacture of semiconductors.
- The third story is about using data and analytics to reduce the time to detect anomalies in manufacturing processing steps.

In contrast to these three stories, a fourth story in this chapter is about using data and analytics, not in manufacturing, but in optimizing a portfolio of hardware products.

Challenge: Scheduling a Complex Manufacturing Process in a Semiconductor Fab

Opened in July 2002, IBM's 300-mm fabrication (fab) facility in Fishkill, New York, was one of the very first fully automated semiconductor plants in the world.[1] Semiconductor processing starts with silicon wafers that are made from very carefully grown cylindrical-shaped silicon crystal that are sliced to a thickness of about 0.75 mm. The wafers are then subjected to a series of manufacturing steps that create electrical features and connections between those features.[2] Semiconductor manufacturing is characterized as "re-entrant flow," meaning that the same sequence of equipment is repeatedly used on a wafer to build layer after layer of circuitry. Scheduling semiconductor lines is difficult, as different products and products at different levels of completion are in contention for the same resources. Using simple rules, such as "first in, first out," "shortest processing time first," and "nearest to completion first" can lead to poor overall utilization of the manufacturing resources.

The silicon wafers used in the Fishkill facility are 300 mm in diameter, which is why the facility is often called the 300-mm fab. This fab is 140,000 square feet in size and includes 200 miles of pipes and tubes and 600 miles of cable and wiring.[3] The fab is used for both new product development and for the manufacturing of mature products. Combining development and manufacturing in one line can significantly reduce time to market for new products. However, the dual use of the line significantly complicates the automation of the line and the scheduling of line resources as the development wafers have a higher priority than the production ones to reduce development time. The manufacturing process involving a wafer includes hundreds of processing steps; some of the most complicated steps are chemical deposition, etching, diffusion, plating, and ion implantation.[4] A single semiconductor device—commonly referred to as a chip—such as a state-of-the-art microprocessor, can have millions of transistors in it, and a single wafer can contain hundreds of chips. After wafer processing and testing are complete, the wafer is cut into individual chips (known as "dicing" the wafer). A major problem IBM needed to solve was how to optimally schedule the manufacturing lines to maximize overall throughput while taking into account the variable priorities of the different types of wafers. In an earlier IBM fab, the manufacturing lines had been scheduled largely by a priority-based scheme, which took into account the expected remaining time in the system from a queuing or simulation model and the due date. A joint team of engineers from IBM's Microelectronics Division and ILOG was formed for scheduling and dispatch. Initially, the team considered queuing theory as a technique for scheduling the work in the 300-mm fab. However, the team soon realized that queuing theory could not capture the complexities of the fab and would not produce adequate results. It needed to deal with many additional intricacies of the facility, including tool usage history and planned maintenance. Without an efficient scheduler for the fab line, raw materials and manufacturing assets may be inefficiently used, and time-sensitive procedures might be delayed.

IBM and ILOG worked jointly to use mixed-integer programming and constraint programming in a special-purpose decomposition algorithm for the scheduling of the fab.[5] The software evolved into ILOG Fab PowerOps (FPO), a flexible solution for semiconductor production scheduling. FPO consists of a data model, graphical interfaces, and an optimization engine based on ILOG CPLEX.[6] FPO provides a comprehensive scheduling solution for the 300-mm fab by allocating groups of wafers (known as FOUPs) to processing machines for photolithography, diffusion, etching, thin films, and implants—in an optimal sequence of processes. FPO was used to develop the near real-time dynamic planning system for IBM's 300-mm fab.[7] Existing business rules are supported by the solution, creating optimal manufacturing schedules that are executed automatically. To create an optimal schedule, the software replans an entire day of production approximately every five minutes. The solution helps optimize the utilization of a number of different tools used in the fab, including furnaces, wet tools, and lithography tools. The optimization can take into account a variety of constraints, including throughput or new business priorities. The solution also has an interface that users can use to investigate, analyze, and fine-tune aspects of the scheduler.

When asked about the use of ILOG FPO for manufacturing, Pierre Haren, then Chairman and CEO, ILOG, replied, "For varied processes around the world, this solution minimizes machine idle waiting time and optimizes the flow of material in the plant, so in a sense, we make the world hum rather than hiccup."

One of the early challenges with the deployment of the FPO software was getting the manufacturing line employees to follow the computed schedule when it produced instructions to leave a tool idle for a time, when there was work available that the tool could do. Such instructions arise when the software has evaluated many alternatives and has determined that it is better for the tool to wait for a short period of time for additional or alternate work to arrive than to begin to process available work. In a sense, the computer was playing chess three moves ahead of its human counterpart, and this required explanation. The ILOG team learned that providing a graphical explanation, such as a Gantt chart for an idle period, helped with adoption. For example, when a manufacturing line worker realized that while the processing of 50 low-priority wafers might be briefly delayed if the tool remained idle for 5 minutes, 100 high-priority wafers could be processed without serious impact on the delivery date of the initial 50 wafers. The ILOG schedule combines a "big-picture" view with a view of all the many details of hundreds of process-ing steps.

Outcome: Reduced Production Times

The ILOG solution is credited with a 15% reduction in production times.[8] The solution also reduced the overhead required to adapt to changing circumstances. *Semiconductor International* awarded IBM the 2005 Top Fab of the Year.[9] Peter Singer, Editor-in-Chief of *Semiconductor International*, was impressed by the "first-time right" track record of IBM's 300-mm fab.[10] ILOG FPO is responsible for getting the schedule right the first time.

Analytics is also used to enhance the yield and improve the quality control of the chips produced in IBM's 300-mm fab. The fab is highly instrumented and has been collecting big data since before the term became ubiquitous.

Challenge: Enhancing Yield in the Manufacturing of Semiconductors

In 2005, Bernie Meyerson, IBM Fellow, and Brenda Dietrich realized that IBM was not exploiting the full potential of the vast amount of data it was collecting in the 300-mm fab. Different people were looking at different data sets for different business purposes. Some engineers were looking at final product performance, such as individual microprocessor speeds. Others were looking at data in very fine detail, such as studying the size of a certain fea-ture that was created by using photolithography on the wafers. Dietrich offered her math department to help aggregate and apply data mining tech-niques to the data from the fab. Once an agreement to collaborate was reached, Robert Baseman, Senior Technical Staff Member, IBM Research, was assigned the responsibility. Baseman seized the opportunity to aggregate data and apply data mining techniques for overall yield improvement in semicon-ductor manufacturing. Baseman, along with other scientists from IBM Research and engineers from IBM's Systems and Technology Group, built a portfolio of advanced analytics solutions to enhance yield and improve qual-ity control. One of the solutions, **Enhanced Data Mining**, is used to identify specific tools and processes and combinations with significant influences on critical manufacturing yield and product quality measures.[11]

In order to produce the volume of chips demanded, the fab operates as many as 50 nominally identical processing chambers for some processing steps. In addition, many of these processing chambers are capable of perform-ing multiple processing steps. The large number of chambers, flexibility in chamber use, highly re-entrant flow in the fab, and range of products results in an extremely complicated production logistics history. In a relatively short period of time, the fab might use tens of thousands of chamber and process combinations. The exact sequence of tools used, the status of a chamber in its maintenance cycle, and even the choice of chambers or positions within a tool, may potentially cause a variation in the characteristics of the end product, which is generally undesirable. Certain critical final product measures must be kept within very small ranges. A microprocessor, for example, must be fast enough to meet the specifications of the product it will be used in but not so fast that it draws more power than planned for in the end product's design. Being able to accurately predict and control the speed of microprocessors is essential.

Enhanced Data Mining focuses on a relatively small number—typically dozens—of critical measurements of the final product characteristics. The solution detects processing chambers and combinations of chambers that are associated with aberrations in some critical characteristic of the wafer. For example, if 10 chambers are supposed to be doing the same thing but measurements show that the yield of wafers from 9 of the chambers is 80% and the yield from the tenth chamber is only 60%, then the tenth chamber needs to be investigated. Identifying the aberrant chambers early allows engineers to take remedial action, which reduces cost and waste.

The solution uses a binary recursive tree algorithm to search the production logistics data to find patterns; it incorporates proprietary methods to generalize and extract rules from data mining trees to optimize impact and ease of use. Some of these methods ensure that signals delivered to the engineers are not merely statistically significant but have genuine operational or practical significance. The solution also provides investigating engineers confirming data reports, facilitating root cause analysis, which is critical to successful solution adoption.

The big data from the manufacturing process is an example of two of the four big data Vs: *Volume*, because of the large volume of data, and *Velocity*, because some of the data is processed in near real time.[12] For the majority of processes, the fault detection and classification system analyzes a selected subset of the trace data collected during wafer processing in near real time. If sufficiently abnormal behavior is detected, the system can prevent the tools from processing additional wafers.

Outcome: Cost Savings Due to Yield Improvement

IBM pursued dozens of the diagnoses of aberrant chamber behavior affecting yields from Enhanced Data Mining, and as a result, it realized a cost savings well in excess of $1 million.[13] Moreover, using analytics to improve chip yields, detect problems before they become problems, and optimize the manufacturing process has resulted in $21 million of annual incremental revenue and $32 million in annual cost savings.[14]

Challenge: Reducing the Time to Detect Aberrant Events

While the analysis of production logistics history reveals many opportunities for yield enhancement, those analyses require chips to progress in the manufacturing process until the critical measurements are made and so aberrations in processing may not be detected as rapidly as desired. Most processing chambers are equipped with hundreds of chemical, physical, and mechanical sensors that collect data while wafers are being processed. Analysis of this so-called process trace data presents an opportunity to dramatically reduce the time to detect aberrant behaviors.

The fab's real-time control system monitors a small fraction of the process trace data and will inhibit a tool if significantly abnormal behavior is detected, but the vast majority of the process trace data was not analyzed proactively. Baseman's team from IBM Research built the **Tracer Framework** to support the development of off-line analyses of the entirety of the process trace data.[15]

The complex nature of the trace data presents multiple analytical challenges:

- There are many different kinds of aberration signatures to be detected.
- A plethora of possible events drive aberrant behavior; there are inherent data mismatches between some nominally identical chambers.
- The data is highly non-normal, and there are large numbers of statistically significant but operationally insignificant aberrations.

In addition, the team faced challenges in preprocessing the data for analysis. The tool set in IBM's 300-mm fab evolves rapidly, in response to the dynamic demands of its joint production and development mission. As a result, while vast amounts of data have been generated by the fab, much of that data is not immediately suitable for analysis. For example, some newer tools have sensors that older tools do not have, different tool groups or products may use different naming conventions, and there may be differences in the calibrations of the sensors. All these differences must be rationalized somehow to ultimately aggregate the data collected by different tools. In addition, there may be erroneous measurements where a machine is behaving badly, making it necessary to identify the outliers.

While working with engineers in the fab, the team learned what additional data the engineers considered when evaluating a finding from Tracer. The team also learned what graphs or visuals were most effective in causing an engineer to take an action. Dynamic reference data was built into the analytics in Tracer so that when a manufacturing tool shows aberrant behavior, an engineer can easily look at short-term and long-term data about that tool, as well as at similar data for other tools. Tracer analyses incorporated inventive use of nonparametric and robust information-theoretic methods and have detected numerous tool instabilities and mismatches associated with aging components, maintenance events, and new product process introductions.

Figure 8-1 shows an example of informative data that an engineer can evaluate before taking action. This data is from one particular sensor, sensor 19, during one step, step 24, of a particular processing recipe from all of the nominally identical tools (chambers) performing that process. The data from the chamber in question is stable and well matched to the data from the other chambers from month/day 9/6 through 10/2. An arrow at the top of the right graph indicates an anomaly at month/day 10/4. This value for this chamber on 10/4 is more than 30,000, which is much higher than the other data points, indicating a dramatic shift in the behavior of this chamber. (To see a color version of this figure, go to www.ibmpressbooks.com/title/9780133833034.)

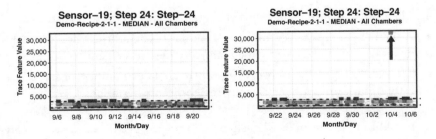

Figure 8-1   Visualization of sensor data from multiple chambers

Outcome: Engineers Take Action

Engineers reported that they have taken action on more than 1,000 findings generated by Tracer.

Challenge: Simplifying the Hardware Product Portfolio

As part of the company's transformation to a globally integrated enterprise,[16] IBM has formed organizational structures to support execution of specific aspects of the transformation. These structures are called Enterprise Transformation Initiatives (ETIs). To simplify IBM's hardware product portfolio, the Hardware Product Management Transformation (HPMT) ETI was launched in 2007. This initiative is currently led by Cary Dollard, Vice President of Technical Operations, IBM Systems and Technology Group. The objective of this ETI is to reduce the complexity of the hardware portfolio to enable cost and expense savings for IBM and, at the same time, to simplify the product offerings for IBM customers.

A product portfolio has numerous disparate pieces of information that need to be accumulated and rationalized together. Questions to answer include:

- What are the unique hardware configurations—specific machines and models—in the portfolio today?
- What is the financial performance (current results) of the unique machine configurations?
- What unique options and features are associated with these products?
- What is the volume performance associated with these unique options and features?
- How are the products performing in the current year compared to their current operation plan?
- How are the products performing compared to their product life cycle plan (multiyear)?

One of the early challenges was that *all* the product data was not centrally located. Using detailed analysis, key aspects of all unique products were accumulated in a data mart. This data included unique product hardware and clones, announcement dates, withdrawal dates, volumes, and financial performance. Once the data is centrally located and available, Cognos is used to pull data for quarterly reports for the general managers to show them different views of revenue, margin, profit, and volume for their products. Some product managers had not previously had a comprehensive view of the data about their product because pulling the data together from so many sources was complicated. The HPMT team learned that when data can be viewed in aggregate, data trends become more obvious and meaningful.

As with any other transformational project, some things in this project worked well, and others did not. In one example, IBM Research joined the HPMT team to create the Portfolio Analyzer tool, which considers all of the known data about a product, including the forecasted information. Portfolio Analyzer then uses a number of predictive algorithms to provide recommendations for actions to take on the portfolio. The team used this tool to make projections about product life cycles to estimate which products to sell and which products to eliminate, based on cost and profit projections. Unfortunately, the tool normally recommended selling only high-margin products, which would result in significant gaps in IBM's target hardware market coverage, which includes some low-end products. The tool concept was valid, but because some business constraints were not included in the model, the output was not useful. The HPMT team found that deep-dive analysis on specific products captured relevant data more accurately. This analysis was used to recommend changes with the product managers.

Transformational changes can be challenging. Users need to be able to see specifically what benefit will be derived from implementing recommended changes. The HPMT team found that the following factors ensure success:

- Fact-based data and metrics are essential.
- It's important to get executive champion(s) buy-in and support.
- It's important to get finance and subject matter experts for the products involved early.
- Thinking "end to end" about benefit and costs is beneficial.
- A feedback loop was created for future product improvements.

Outcome: Significant Reduction of Hardware Product Portfolio

The HPMT initiative has provided product managers with comprehensive and valuable data that they were previously not able to get. The best indicator of the success of the HPMT initiative is that the number of unique systems has been reduced by 50% and the objective of having the optimal portfolio has been achieved. Portfolio changes year to year are less than 5% as older products are removed from the portfolio when new products are announced.

Lessons Learned

Adoption of analytics results is enabled by explaining how the results were obtained. In the 300-mm fab, when the scheduling system recommended that a tool be idle, manufacturing line staff needed an explanation, especially in the early phases of deployment. The HPMT team learned that it needed fact-based analysis to explain how it arrived at a recommended action for a product portfolio so that the product owners would be willing to follow the recommendation.

For analytics results to be more consumable, they need to be put in the context of the end user. The Tracer team discovered that to compel engineers to act on the team's diagnosis, it had to make it easy for the engineers to explore additional data; the team determined the best chart or visual to use to best convey their diagnosis.

Relationships inferred from data today may not be present in data collected tomorrow. The data collected in the 300-mm fab represents the performance of the fab at the time the data was collected. The state of the manufacturing equipment changes with time and usage. For example, data collected about the performance of a chamber in a tool may indicate good performance one day and have an aberration on another day.

Fast, cheap processors and cheap storage make analysis on big data possible. Now that processors and data storage are inexpensive, performing analytics on the vast amount of data from the 300-mm fab is not only practical but imperative.

It's important to leverage the levers. As discussed in Chapter 1, "Why Big Data and Analytics?" organizations that excel at leveraging the nine levers of differentiation are deriving the most value from data and analytics.[17] The Systems and Technology Group has made good use of several of the nine levers. The availability and use of data and the structure and formality of data governance both from the 300-mm fab and in the portfolio analysis of products is evidence of two of the levers: *Culture* and *Data*. Other levers that the Systems and Technology Group leverages include *Measurement*, *Source of Value*, *Sponsorship*, and *Trust*. These levers are helping the group realize value from its big data.

Endnotes

1. "IBM CEO Palmisano, N.Y. Gov. Pataki Unveil IBM 300mm Chip Facility," IBM News Room—News Releases, July 2002. http://www-03.ibm.com/press/us/en/pressrelease/584.wss.

2. "IBM Power7 300mm wafer," IBM News Room—Image Gallery, February 2010. http://www-03.ibm.com/press/us/en/photo/29338.wss.

3. "IBM CEO Palmisano, N.Y. Gov. Pataki Unveil IBM 300mm Chip Facility."

4. Van Zant, P., *Microchip Fabrication*, 5th edition, McGraw-Hill Professional, May 2004.

5. Fordyce, K., Bixby, R., and Burda, R., "Technology That Upsets the Social Order—A Paradigm Shift in Assigning Lots to Tools in a Wafer Fabricator—The Transition from Rules to Optimization," *Proceedings of the 2008 Winter Simulation Conference*. http://www.informs-sim.org/wsc08papers/284.pdf.

6. Buecker, A., et al., "Optimization and Decision Support Design Guide—Using IBM ILOG Optimization Decision Manager," *IBM Redbook*, October 2012. http://www.redbooks.ibm.com/redbooks/pdfs/sg248017.pdf.

7. Peters, S., "ILOG Signs Agreement with IBM for Semiconductor Solutions," December 19, 2006. https://ajax.sys-con.com/node/315895/mobile.

8. Mayhew-Smith, A., "IBM Agrees to Demo ILOG Fab Software at Fishkill," *ElectronicsWeekly.com*, December 19, 2006. http://www.electronicsweekly.com/news/research/process-rd/ibm-agrees-to-demo-ilog-fab-software-at-fishkill-2006-12/.

9. "Semiconductor International Announces 2005 Top Fab of the Year Award Winner," *PR Newswire*, December 1, 2005. http://www.prnewswire.com/news-releases/semiconductor-international-announces-2005-top-fab-of-the-year-award-winner-55140227.html.

10. Ibid.

11. Weiss, S. M., et al., "Rule-Based Data Mining for Yield Improvement in Semiconductor Manufacturing," *Applied Intelligence*, Volume 33, 2010. http://rd.springer.com/article/10.1007%2Fs10489-009-0168-9#page-1.

12. Schroeck, M., et al., "Analytics: The Real-World Use of Big Data—How Innovative Enterprises Extract Value from Uncertain Data," IBM Institute for Business Value, October 2012. http://www-03.ibm.com/systems/hu/resources/the_real_word_use_of_big_data.pdf.

13. Weiss, S. M., et al., "Rule-Based Data Mining for Yield Improvement in Semiconductor Manufacturing."

14. Sanford, L., "The Road to a Smarter Enterprise: Six Principles to Consider," FWSIM CIO Executive Leadership Summit, October 25, 2010.

15. Bagchi, S., et al., "Data Analytics and Stochastic Modeling in a Semiconductor Fab," *Applied Stochastic Models in Business and Industry*, Volume 26, Issue 1, January 2010. http://dl.acm.org/citation.cfm?id= 1753052.
16. Palmisano, S., "The Globally Integrated Enterprise," *Foreign Affairs*, May/June 2006. http://www.foreignaffairs.com/articles/61713/samuel-j-palmisano/the-globally-integrated-enterprise.
17. Balboni, F., et al., "Analytics: A Blueprint for Value—Converting Big Data and Analytics into Results," IBM Institute for Business Value, November 2013. http://public.dhe.ibm.com/common/ssi/ecm/en/gbe03575usen/GBE03575USEN.PDF.

9

Increasing Sales Performance

"The positive correlation between online commerce enablement and wallet share is at least as much a statement of the potential downside risk from falling behind as it is a statement of the potential upside from leading in the market."

—David Bush, Senior Managing Consultant, Global Business Services Strategy and Change Internal Practice, IBM Corporation

Perspective: Using Analytics to Optimize Sales Performance–Inside and Out

The traditional roles of buyers and sellers have undergone a significant shift as access to information has increased. Buyers can easily search on the web for reviews and recommendations from other buyers and use the information they find as input to their purchasing decisions. That same trend expands beyond the business-to-consumer (B2C) model. Business-to-business (B2B) buyers have also undergone a significant power shift over the past few years, which in turn is driving a transformation in sales organizations. Sophisticated buyers research the products or solutions, check reviews using social tools to get peer recommendations, and come to the buying process armed with insights and information. Sellers once provided that type of information and now have to find new ways to add value. What today's sophisticated buyers need from sales personnel is more consultative selling that focuses on *their* business problem or opportunity and how to address it most effectively.

According to the Corporate Executive Board Sales Leadership report, "Today's buyer sophistication is forcing sales organizations to transform how they sell. The standard response from sales leaders has been to build and drive adherence to new seller skills. However, this approach is insufficient for driving change in a new selling environment characterized by customers' increased access to information, where in order to be successful reps must be able to exercise judgment throughout the commercial process."[1]

Analytics plays an important role in the transformation of sales organizations. As sellers need to exercise more judgment throughout the process, analytics can provide fact-based analysis to enable the consultative approach to selling. Sales management can leverage analytics to optimize coverage for accounts and analyze buying patterns. Analytics also informs sellers of client purchasing behavior and the benefits of moving toward digital commerce for B2B commerce.

How IBM Approached Leveraging Analytics in Sales Organizations

One challenge most companies face is aligning the right sales resources to the best opportunities for generating revenue. IBM has approximately 450,000 employees in 170 countries and a large sales force supporting a portfolio of more than 2,000 hardware and software offerings and more than 1,000 services offerings. Improving the effectiveness and productivity of such a large sales force can have a significant impact on both revenue growth and cost savings. Coverage decisions regarding assigning sales staff to accounts, products, or territories are often based on past revenue. Such a backward-looking process can miss significant revenue growth opportunities. With the use of predictive analytics and big data, the possibilities for addressing the coverage challenge are expanding.

In 2005 IBM initiated the **Market Alignment Program (MAP)** to "optimally allocate sales resources based on field-validated analytics estimates of future revenue opportunities in operational market segments."[2] OnTarget is a prospecting sales tool that increases seller efficiency. Prospects identified by OnTarget were converted to opportunities at more than twice the rate of prospects not targeted by this system. These two projects helped generate an estimated $1 billion in incremental revenue in their first three years of use and were nominated for the Franz Edelman Award for achievement in operations research.[3]

The Business Performance Services team, under Martin Fleming, Vice President, Business Performance Services and IBM Chief Economist, was formed to take on large-scale analytics projects for IBM. Of significance, several of these projects have been focused on improving sales performance through an improved sales coverage model. Business Performance Services undertook the **Territory Optimization Program (TOP)** to support sales managers' decision processes. The **Coverage Optimization with Profitability (COP)** project is a recent example of the continuing innovation that uses analytics to improve business outcomes.

Analytics can be leveraged in many other ways to support an increase in sales performance, and IBM has been creatively working in several areas to do so. The **Watson Sales Assistant** project discussed in Chapter 5, "Enabling Analytics Through Information Technology," uses the technology that won the *Jeopardy!* television game to help provide sellers with answers to questions that they and their clients have about IBM's extensive portfolio of offerings.

Using Analytics to Build a Business Case for Inside Sales

Another rigorous analytics project built a business case for investing in new modern digital commerce capabilities. The "Online Commerce" section of this chapter describes the analytics approach taken to successfully build the business case that resulted in a new Enterprise Transformation Initiative (ETI) that was largely driven by client demand. While many of the transformational analytics stories are internally motivated, the Smarter Commerce Inside IBM—Sell-Side ETI is the direct result of chief procurement officers' (CPOs') growing demand to transact digitally with preferred suppliers. IBM intends to use its capability to fully integrate and enable end-to-end purchasing automation for clients as a strategic differentiator in delivering a "signature client experience." The Inside Sales organization has taken on this challenge and is racing to gain the advantage that early providers of this capability will have. IBM expects online commerce, or digitally enabled revenue, to grow more than 150% by 2015. The shift in client preference for some sales tasks to be handled electronically is at the foundation of the strategy developed by the Smarter Commerce Inside IBM—Sell-Side ETI discussed in the "Online Commerce" section of this chapter.

While the examples in this chapter are discussed in separate sections, it is important to note that the interrelationship across them is key to the sales transformation process. Figure 9-1 depicts the synergy of the projects to drive sales outcomes. IBM uses analytics across the end-to-end process to transform sales. For example, the Market Alignment Program (MAP) is used in the *Identify opportunity and prioritize clients* and *Differentiate go-to-market by client segment* steps. TOP is used in the *Assign sales resources* step, and COP is used across those three steps in the process, providing profitability insight for client segmentation, data for potential resource shifts, and insights to sales leaders to influence territory setting and to monitor shifts and measure impact. The examples highlighted in this chapter are part of an overall framework that is driving sales transformation. Analytics projects are underway across this framework. The examples that follow are from the first three steps.

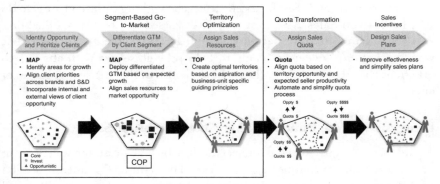

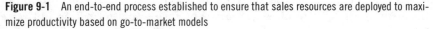

Figure 9-1   An end-to-end process established to ensure that sales resources are deployed to maximize productivity based on go-to-market models

Challenge: Deploying Sellers for Maximum Revenue Growth by Account

MAP was designed to address the business challenge of deploying sellers to accounts with potential higher future revenue rather than leaving them on accounts with historically high revenue. MAP provides a bottom-up view of market allocation. This analytically informed approach contrasts with the conventional way of assigning sellers based on recent revenue or historical spending. It is a forward-looking assessment that incorporates a realistic revenue opportunity assessment for each large client. This assessment, essentially an estimate of the information technology spending by the client, is then decomposed into the amount of specific product group that IBM would potentially be able to sell to that account. It was important to decompose spending to the specific product group level in order to assign the correctly skilled sales resources to cover the opportunity.

A significant challenge in the project was matching each company listed in the IBM internal database to the equivalent entry in external databases such as Dun & Bradstreet. This involved assessing millions of companies worldwide. The company needed to reconcile subsidiaries and other complex business model organizations for each of the modeled clients.

According to Lawrence, "Taking a high-level statement of a set of business objectives and refining them into a well-defined analytics problem that optimization approaches or predictive-modeling algorithms can address is a major challenge in the modeling process."[4] In addressing a challenge of such large scope, MAP had to analyze massive amounts of data in order to "yield a relatively small set of explanatory features that are used as direct input to the predictive algorithm."[5]

Prior to the development of MAP, the process of estimating forward-looking revenue growth at the account level relied only on historical data and field sales assessments, and thus it was typically correlated with the size and composition of the sales team previously assigned to the account. MAP took the approach of generating a view of the potential revenue that might be generated if sales efforts were intensified or modified. It considered what revenue could be rather than what it had been.

The MAP process consisted of three key steps. The first step was the development of the analytics model to produce estimates of revenue by IBM product groups at each account. The second step was to validate that model with the field sales force through a series of workshops. Hundreds of workshops were held, each with a particular product group or sales territory. The third step was to reallocate sales resources based on where the analysis indicated an imbalance between the estimated revenue potential and the current sales resources. According to Lawrence, during the workshop, the analytics estimates were used as an "objective starting point. The sales team could either accept the model results or provide modified numbers and reasons for modifying them." This process exercised the *Data* lever outlined in Chapter 1, "Why Big Data and Analytics?" by engaging with the sales teams. Incorporating sales assessments based on the fact-driven analytics estimate built organizational confidence in the process. This confidence was critical to driving value through the use of MAP. The *Culture* lever was also demonstrated in the MAP approach as introducing the availability and use of analytics to drive the allocation of resources; it was a significant change to the conventional approach and decision process.

The discussions around revenue centered on three important estimates: total IT spending by product group, total attainable opportunity for the customer, and "realistically attainable" assessment.

Outcome: Increased Sales Performance

In order to drive outcomes, the MAP project, like any other analytics project, had to create a way for decision makers to easily consume the insights produced by the predictive model. MAP designed web-based tools for use by sales managers in order to deliver the recommendations and insights for their sales resource alignment decisions. The ability to embed analytics into a decision process is one way to ensure that value can be amplified.

MAP was able to provide fact-based objective assessments, which helps minimize the natural human bias that often goes into forward-looking estimates about accounts and about sales teams. Analytics was needed to accomplish this, given the scale of the 25 brands plus service offerings that it covered. Sales teams that aligned their account resources with MAP recommendations outperformed the other IBM sales teams by 7%. MAP successfully identified nearly $22 billion of investment account opportunity potential for IBM to pursue. Over a four-year period, MAP contributed $1 billion in revenue.[6]

Another valuable outcome of MAP is that the aspirational revenue data from it was used in another initiative, COP (also covered in this chapter), thereby scaling the impact of the project to drive increased value.

Challenge: Deploying Sellers Within a Territory

The challenge TOP addresses is to increase sales productivity and drive incremental revenue growth within a sales territory. TOP is designed for use by sales managers to create optimal territories of accounts and to assign sales resources to cover the territories. Giving sales managers the capability to automatically optimize the design of their territories would increase sales productivity and effectiveness. Matt Callahan, IBM Director, Sales Coverage and Transformation, explains that what TOP is really about is helping sales managers see how their teams are currently deployed and then helping them make better decisions about the future deployment of each of the sales representatives.

Market opportunity, client segmentation, and industry specialization are all factors that go into this decision process. With TOP, sales managers can use fact-based analytics to gain insights into current staff assignments, work load, and market opportunity in order to define the most effective territories.

TOP relied on two fundamental universes of data: one with information about IBM clients and the other with information about IBM sellers. Data about the existing IBM clients was sourced at the transactional level from the financial systems ledger. Every sales transaction hits the ledger, and every transaction is associated with a specific customer number representing the buying entity. There are often multiple buying entities within a single client account, so transactions must be aggregated from customer numbers up to a client ID to give an accurate view of the total IBM revenue from a client. This was one of the most challenging parts of the data preparation phase for the project, as it was critical to be able to aggregate individual transactions into a single named client.

The next step was to use the sales data to extract descriptive statistics about the sales staff, such as number of industries each seller covers, number of clients each seller covers, and total opportunity each seller covers. Building the model based on those characteristics was important in comparing revenue, diversity, and opportunities available to each seller. Once that view was built for every seller, scorecards could be built to show sales leaders in a region the actual measurements in comparison to guiding principles that would help optimize the territory. For example, when the Software Group wanted to be aligned by industry, it could examine the descriptive statistics for software sellers and see how well the coverage mapped to that objective in a particular country or region.

When data was presented to sales managers, they could take the guiding principle (for example, align by industry) and look at segments that were not well aligned according to that principle. Then given their clients, their sales resources, and the guiding principles, the model could recommend an optimal approach, opening up possibilities that may not have been considered before. IBM Research built algorithms to develop the recommended territory optimization. The project used IBM Cognos, WebSphere®, and DB2®.

Outcome: Increased Territory Performance

TOP is available across IBM to assist in the process of optimizing territories. Territories that follow TOP recommendations have been shown to outperform those that do not by an average of 10%. TOP worked two levers:[7] *Source of Value*, providing a tool to support sales territory decisions, and

Measurement, by evaluating the impact on business outcomes. The CIO Lab and Global Business Services have continued to work with TOP application and have used IBM WebSphere operational decision management software for implementation.

Challenge: Determining the Optimal Sales Coverage Investment by Account

COP is a big data application that is delivering results. The challenge was to understand at an account level the sales expense associated with the revenue generated. Once this association was computed from the data, the tool also provided a recommendation for either increasing, maintaining, or decreasing the sales resources associated with an account. Big data is used to create a view of the revenue, gross margin, and profitability of the IBM sales team at an account level. There are more than 200 million rows of data used to produce a three-year historical view of each account as well as a two-year future projection. The data comes together in the Research Cloud, and IBM SPSS and Cognos are used for the analysis. The team is migrating to a PureSystems environment to increase performance of this data-intensive solution. COP segments the clients by their profit margins: high, medium, low, and negative. The thresholds for high, medium, and low are defined based on average geographic and brand profit margin for the past three years. For example, profit margin for a client in Software group (SWG) France is considered high if it's above average SWG France profit margin for the previous three years.

COP started with a request from senior executives who wanted to understand the sales, general, and administrative (SG&A) expense at a client level in order to make coverage recommendations. To do so, an approach had to be developed to assess how sellers and other sales resources were investing their time. COP was designed to support the sales leader decision process and not to make the decisions for them. That was a key distinction that had to be communicated to the sales leaders. Many times COP is considered a sales coverage recommendation engine similar to Amazon for IBM sales leaders.

The process to start COP followed a standard project decomposition approach that the Business Performance Services (BPS) team uses. First, the team had to understand at which accounts the sellers were spending their time, so they started to think about "How can we measure that? What are the different data sources available?" From there, the data sources were identified as the sales activity (customer relationship management) systems,

Siebel and Sales Connect. In addition to those sources there were many others, some of which were unique to particular business units. The challenge was to take the many available data sources and determine how the data could be turned into a measure of time spent at a client.

Once the team had handled that challenge, the next was to develop an estimate of the sales cost at the account level. The goal was not to get to 100% accuracy, as the recommendations would be at an account level and would be directional input to the sales managers.

With the data gathered and analyzed, the team had an informed view of sales resource and cost at the account level. The next step was to look at all the pieces of the data as input to a model that would produce an understandable recommendation that was not too complex. As the team got deeper into the project, it found that it was using massive amounts of data, doing a vast array of calculations on hundreds of millions of rows. Usability is extremely important, and you don't have to understand analytics technology to make effective use of the results analytics produces. The sales managers who would use the output of COP would not need to understand the algorithms that produced those recommendations. To be effective, the team had to wrap the math calculations in the language and the process of the sales manager. With the massive amount of data used, the senior stakeholders in the reviews would comment, "This is extremely interesting and useful stuff, but how are you going to make this actionable? What are you going to do with it?" according to COP Program Manager Nick Otto, IBM Executive Program Manager, Business Performance Services. Otto said that the issue of usability drove their thinking, and they engaged IBM Research to address this issue. The challenge was to reconcile massive amounts of data containing a lot of very insightful knowledge with something easily understood that could be given to the sales teams to drive value for IBM. That part of the challenge is where the team spent the majority of its time. It was clear that the levers outlined in Chapter 1 were being put to good use throughout COP. The *Measurement* lever was used as the team leveraged big data to measure account sales expense. The *Source of Value* lever was apparent in the recommendations that the model made to support coverage decisions and help maximize profitability from the sales allocations. Because a lot of qualitative insight goes into sales, initial discussions with sales leaders could be hostile or skeptical. The model provided an objective data-driven basis to start the discussion, and qualitative insight was used to make the decision. Figure 9-2 shows the high-level recommendations based on the model.

	High Revenue Growth		Low Revenue Growth	
Profit Margin	1. High Opportunity Headroom	2. Low Opportunity Headroom	3. High Opportunity Headroom	4. Low Opportunity Headroom
A. High	Increase	Increase	Increase	Maintain
B. Medium	Increase	Maintain	Maintain	Maintain
C. Low	Maintain	Decrease	Decrease	Decrease
D. Very Low	Decrease	Decrease	Decrease	Decrease

Figure 9-2   COP nets results down to three recommendations: increase, maintain, or decrease the sales resource investment

Outcome: Increased Revenue and Increased Productivity

Between 2011 and the end of 2013, COP had already produced millions of dollars in revenue growth. It is a strategic ETI that drives very prescriptive actions. It has proven very successful in its recommendations and is becoming part of the culture of the Sales organization. Pilot teams that aligned with the COP recommendations saw a 90% increase in revenue and a 70% increase in productivity in those accounts.

Multiple analytics projects across IBM have leveraged COP data. For example, another project leverages COP data at the opportunity level to understand which sales teams drive optimal win rates for different types of deals and clients. The Smarter Commerce Inside IBM—Sell-Side ETI discussed in this chapter leverages COP data to study productivity differences on clients leveraging Smarter Commerce techniques for digital commerce versus those that do not. Another ETI uses COP data to understand the productivity advantages of using tools. The data allows these functions to get a granular, quantified view of productivity gains, which drives value for the business. Being able to fully understand and measure client-by-client productivity net of sales expense is the key to unlocking additional insights. Scaling impact of analytics projects can only occur when there is an openness to share and collaborate across different groups; this drives maximum value for the company.

Online Commerce

B2B sales organizations are increasingly prioritizing investments for inside sales (sometimes referred to as *telesales*).[8] While inside sales can significantly reduce costs and improve efficiency, another significant driver of this trend is that buyers themselves have become more comfortable with "purchasing and collaborating remotely; they use the web to research product information, are comfortable communicating and collaborating with sellers using methods such as email, social media, and conference calls, and in fact prefer these methods over face-to-face communication for some sales tasks."[9]

At IBM the Online Commerce organization has gone a step further: In addition to ramping up inside sellers and using analytics and social media tools to drive effectiveness and revenue, another team within the organization is focusing on specialized online commerce solutions that are being driven by clients—in particular, CPOs. Within IBM, *online commerce enablement* refers to the process of electronically enabling a client's procure-to-pay processes with IBM.

The CPO role has been undergoing a transformation that is now driving a corresponding part of IBM's internal transformation. CPOs are negotiating value and not just price. IBM's Institute for Business Value (IBV) and Oxford Economics conducted a comprehensive study to gain insights from CPOs. A total of 1,128 CPOs from 22 countries, each with annual revenue in excess of US$1 billion, were surveyed. The findings showed that companies with top-performing procurement organizations report a 22% higher profit margin than companies with low-performing procurement organizations and 15% higher than the average company.[10]

The CPO works closely with the chief financial officer (CFO), line of business executive, and chief information officer (CIO) in a "four in the box" purchasing model. They are driving increased efficiencies and internal compliance in the purchasing process with suppliers in order to increase value and reduce costs. Patricia Spugani, IBM Program Director, Global Online Commerce Strategy, IBM Inside Sales, and David E. Bush, Senior Managing Consultant, IBM Global Business Services Strategy and Change Internal Practice, have been working to break new ground in this area to respond to client demands. While benefits for Procurement transformation have been quantified by companies, industry analysts, and solution providers, the benefits for suppliers to make corresponding investments have not been as well documented. After using analytics to build the business case for funding and resources, the Smarter Commerce Inside IBM—Sell-Side ETI was formed to address the needs of CPOs and line of business teams to simplify the digital purchasing process with IBM.

We look next at how analytics was used to build the business case for this strategic investment in the Smarter Commerce Inside IBM—Sell-Side ETI.

Challenge: Creating a Smarter Commerce B2B Solution to Drive Cross-Company Efficiencies

There were two key aspects to this challenge. Overall, IBM must understand and respond to client demand to drive cross-company efficiencies in its purchasing process with preferred suppliers. The second challenge was to create a compelling business case to build a new integrated smarter commerce solution that would withstand the competition of other internal initiatives vying for funding. The solution would support all brands at an enterprise level in order to optimize IBM's investments and ensure that clients have a common purchasing experience for any IBM brand in any location.

In order to convince the leadership team to accelerate investments in the technology, resources, and organizational structure to electronically enable client e-procurement across enterprises and firewalls, IBM uses analytics to quantify the benefits for the company. Business leaders understood why increased efficiency would be important to the client's buying process since it saves clients time and money, but why should IBM invest in this instead of other initiatives? A top-down approach to analytics was used to determine the relationship of online commerce enablement to multiple revenue and expense drivers for IBM as a supplier.

To help quantify the benefits, the Strategy and Change Internal Practice (SCIP) team, led by Bush, was brought in to work with Maria Rogers, Vice President, Global Online Commerce, and Spugani, the Global Online Commerce Strategy leader. The SCIP team is made up of specialized consultants who are focused on helping IBM with strategy and transformation initiatives.[11]

The COP data mart was an invaluable data source for the analysis to support the business case.

> *"This is a client-driven innovation that goes through the firewall to transform the B2B e-procurement process. You can only realize so much efficiency within the enterprise; to drive increased efficiency, you have to cross walls for cross-company transformation. Smarter Commerce helps our clients and IBM do that."*
>
> **—Patricia Spugani, Program Director, Global Online Commerce Strategy, IBM Inside Sales, IBM Corporation**

Outcome: An Analytics-Based, Client-Focused Business Case Wins Approval

The benefits of this project for IBM were demonstrated by four powerful findings, each of which resulted from using analytics to test a specific hypothesis.

These four key findings were based on diverse data sources that converged to build a compelling business case. Analytics was used to assess the impact of e-participation on four factors: brand seller productivity (E/R), revenue growth rate (IBM Revenue CAGR), wallet share impact, and the percentage of deals win rate. E-participation, or online commerce enablement, is the percentage of IBM direct Sales Revenue transacted electronically with clients.

Figure 9-3 highlights the outcome of the first hypothesis tested, which found that the sales expense to revenue ratio was higher in accounts that had low e-participation. As the e-participation increases, the expense-to-revenue ratio decreases, meaning that sellers are more productive when accounts increase e-participation.

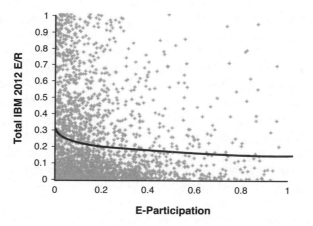

Figure 9-3 Increased e-participation correlates with a lower sales E/R, meaning sellers are more productive when clients have greater e-participation; the statistically significant relationship held after controlling for client worldwide enterprise size

The second hypothesis tested was the impact on the sales expense-to-revenue ratio over time. In order to analyze this, the COP model built by Business Process Services (BPS) was used for the brand seller productivity element. The analytics team found that with increased online commerce enablement, IBM seller expense growth rate stayed neutral, and revenue growth rate increased, as shown in Figure 9-4. This insight was key to understanding that increased e-penetration was a revenue driver rather than a contributor to reduced sales expense.

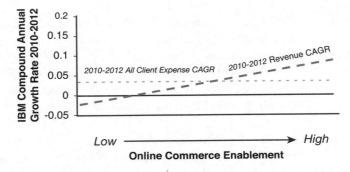

Figure 9-4   With online commerce, revenue growth rate increases while expense growth rate remained neutral

The third hypothesis involved understanding the impact that enabling clients for online commerce had on "wallet share," defined as the percentage of IT spending from the client with IBM compared to the overall estimated enterprise IT spending based on industry IT spending benchmarks and enterprise size data from IBM's Marketing database (MDb). The data showed that online commerce enablement was correlated with an increased share of wallet, as shown in Figure 9-5, providing another proof point that the business case had strong expected quantifiable benefits.

A fourth hypothesis was created to determine whether there was a statistically significant impact on the win rate with increased online commerce enablement. The data shown in Figure 9-6 demonstrates that as the rate of e-penetration, or increased electronic purchasing, increased, the IBM win rate increased as well.

The ETI gained approval from the leadership team based on the anticipated benefits of online commerce as an enabler for the brands' targets. Through this process, the team demonstrated the effective use of the *Source of Value* lever discussed in Chapter 1 by using analytics to inform the actions and decisions to generate value through the new capability of cross-enterprise online commerce. The *Measurement Value* lever was used to demonstrate the correlation between key performance metrics and to validate expected outcomes. The *Sponsorship* lever and *Funding* lever were demonstrated through executive leadership, which used fact-based analysis to make their investment decision and continue to increase funding for the Smarter Commerce Inside IBM—Sell-Side ETI.

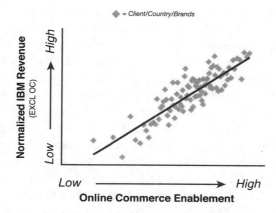

Figure 9-5   Online commerce enablement is correlated with increased share of wallet

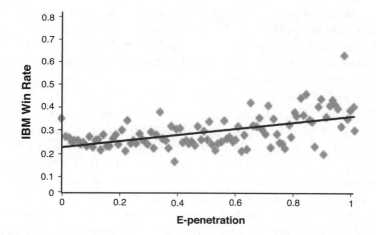

Figure 9-6   Online commerce enablement is correlated with higher IBM win rates

Lessons Learned

You don't have to understand analytics technology to derive value from it. Sales leaders using the recommendations from the COP model did not have to understand big data, the algorithms in the model, or the data sources. They could use the recommendations to increase, maintain, or decrease sales resources in an account to drive value and increase profitability.

The value is realized from the actions taken, not from the insight. To really drive the value, action must be taken on the insight. With the Smarter Commerce Inside IBM—Sell-Side ETI, the analytics drove an investment decision that put into motion the resources to create a new capability to drive increased revenue and loyalty for IBM. As clients find it easier to do business with enabled online commerce across firewalls, it is anticipated that loyalty will also increase. Think about the analogy of a bank account where you pay your bills online, have your paycheck electronically deposited, and have auto pay established. This situation can be thought of as "sticky" because it would take a lot of effort to change banks and start over again. It is the same idea with online commerce: The complexity of B2B transactions leads to more pronounced "stickiness." The new enabled capability to do business the way the CPOs would like to do business and to drive the efficiency improvements through the firewalls would lead to those accounts becoming more loyal.

Relationships inferred from data today may not be present in data collected tomorrow. Big data opens up possibilities to see correlations that were not visible before. It is important to understand that the correlations inferred from the data today may not hold up in the future—unless they are founded in a law of physics or nature. It is important to refresh the models to keep them accurate, as they drive business decisions. New relationships based on new data could change the recommendations.

Sharing and collaborating analytics assets across business units drives maximum value. Data from different analytics initiatives ties together and drives more value. For example, MAP aspirational revenue data is used in the COP model. The COP model and analytics were shared across sales ETIs and enabled several other projects that are driving value for IBM. Through proactive sharing and collaboration with analytics assets, the business is able to scale the impact and drive more results.

It's important to leverage the levers. As discussed in Chapter 1, organizations that excel in leveraging the nine levers of differentiation are deriving the most value from data and analytics. The examples shared in this chapter are just some of the analytics projects under way to help sales, and they engaged the levers *Source of Value*, *Measurement*, and *Culture* in significant ways.

Endnotes

1. "Driving Sales Transformation: Empowering Reps to Sell to Empowered Customers," Corporate Executive Board, December 10, 2013.
2. Lawrence, R., et al., "Operations Research Improves Sales Force Productivity at IBM," *Interfaces*, Volume 40, Number 1, 2010.
3. Ibid.
4. Ibid.
5. Ibid.
6. Sanford, L., "The Road to a Smarter Enterprise: Six Principles to Consider," FWSIM CIO Executive Leadership Summit, October 25, 2010. http://www.google.com/url?sa=t&rct=j&q=&esrc=s&source=web&cd=4&ved=0CEcQFjAD&url=http%3A%2F%2Fwww.hmgstrategy.com%2Fassets%2Fimx%2FPDF%2Fsanford%2520CIO%2520Summit10.25.10_final.ppt&ei=lUbHUtWkHbOgsATSpoHQDQ&usg=AFQjCNFcLStQJQK3mkUAvLV44PUtQ20FSQ&sig2=Ynt-THFokktIuNvF744j5w&bvm=bv.58187178,d.cWc&cad=rja.
7. Balboni, F., et al., "Analytics: A Blueprint for Value—Converting Big Data and Analytics into Results," IBM Institute for Business Value, November 2013. http://public.dhe.ibm.com/common/ssi/ecm/en/gbe03575usen/GBE03575USEN.PDF.
8. Zoltners, A. A., Sinha, P. K., and Lorimer, S. E., "The Growing Power of Inside Sales," *HBR Blog Network*, July 29, 2013, http://blogs.hbr.org/2013/07/the-growing-power-of-inside-sa/.
9. Ibid.
10. LaValle, S., et al., "Analytics: The New Path to Value—How the Smartest Organizations Are Embedding Analytics to Transform Insights into Action," IBM Institute for Business Value, 2010. http://public.dhe.ibm.com/common/ssi/ecm/en/gbe03371usen/GBE03371USEN.PDF.
11. The SCIP team on this project included Josh E. Luber, Stefan R. Cohen, and Ari Papir. The services the team provides internally are similar to the ones that IBM clients hire from Global Business Services.

10

Delivering Services with Excellence

> *"The challenge many enterprises face is to unlock and leverage information that already exists, execute beyond silos of information, and focus on compound business analytics dimensions. For strategic workforce planning, this means integrating information across Human Resources, Operational, and Business Plan dimensions of the business."*
>
> —Daniel D'Elena, Vice President, GBS Worldwide Resource and Capacity Management, Global Business Services, IBM Corporation

Perspective: Leveraging Analytics in a Services Business

Building a competitive consulting business is challenging. Because a consulting business is a talent business, having the right skill at the right time in the right place and utilizing a high percentage of the available resource are necessary for success. Fortunately, consulting is an excellent business in which to leverage analytics to realize business value. Figure 10-1 shows the major steps in a services business, beginning with opportunity identification and ending with a client project to deliver services. The proposal development step also includes consultative selling. As discussed in Chapter 9,

"Increasing Sales Performance," leveraging analytics can increase the performance of sellers across many dimensions. The same techniques can increase performance of consultative sellers, and they are not addressed again here. This chapter focuses on examples of leveraging analytics in four of the steps: opportunity identification, contract signing, resource deployment, and project delivery.

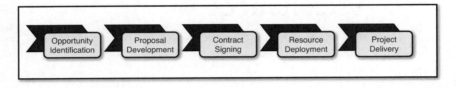

Figure 10-1   Major steps in a services business

For example, data and analytics can improve opportunity identification by providing a near real-time, 360-degree view of potential clients, which gives consultants more current and more complete information about client pain points. After a proposal is accepted, a contract for services is prepared, and analytics can be applied here, too. For example, analytics can be used to predict the risks involved in contracts prior to signing them and suggest risk mitigations. Once a contract is signed, resources need to be assigned to do the work. A services business needs to balance the demand for services with the supply to provide services—namely resources. For example, analytics can be used to predict demand, and optimization can be used to allocate resources to the demand. Once the resources are allocated, work begins on the engagement to develop and deliver services, which may include a solution. During project delivery, there are also opportunities to apply analytics. For example, predictive analytics can be used to predict future risks involved in client projects so that the risks can be mitigated, allowing the projects to deliver services with excellence.

IBM Global Services, formed in 1991, is the world's largest business and technology services provider, operating in more than 170 countries.[1] IBM Global Services consists of two business units: Global Business Services (GBS) and Global Technology Services® (GTS).

GBS has two major capabilities:

- Consulting (strategy, transformation, and system integration)
- Application Management Services (application management, maintenance, and support)

GTS has three major capabilities:

- Information Technology Services (optimization of IT environments)
- Business Process Services (business process platforms and business process outsourcing)
- Strategic Outsourcing Services (transformation of existing infrastructures to deliver improved quality and value)

Each of the GBS and GTS capabilities has a large number of offerings. In 2013, GBS generated $18.4 billion in revenue, with a gross margin of 30.9%, and GTS generated $38.6 billion in revenue, with a gross martin of 38.1%.[2] IBM had more than 400,000 employees in 2013[3]; a significant number of these were in GBS or GTS. Because resources from a very large pool of employees are assigned to deliver a large number of different offerings, there are many opportunities to leverage analytics and optimization for business value. This chapter discusses four of the many examples of the opportunities to leverage analytics: identifying top pursuits, predicting contract risk, enhancing workforce performance, and predicting client project performance.

Challenge: Developing New Business

Prioritizing opportunities according to their likelihood to lead to a sale is important in a services business. Going further—to develop business in new areas—is also important. GTS and IBM Research developed the **Long-Term Signings (LTS)** platform, which supports long-term services business development. LTS is a web-based, big data analytics platform, which integrates information from more than 30 internal and external data sources, such as IBM Connections, financial databases, and LinkedIn, and it provides a near real-time, 360-degree view of companies. For example, data from LinkedIn can be used to find decision makers, such as a chief marketing officer in a company, and the internal data in IBM Connections can determine the best path to reach the decision makers; official reporting structures may not be enough to capture knowledge about a client, since people may change roles or their knowledge may not be visible in an organizational chart. The industry-specific benchmarking feature of LTS is also broadly used in the assessment of existing opportunities in order to further qualify or disqualify them.

Text analytics and predictive analytics are used to profile clients. Entity analytics is used to reconcile customer records. IBM Research developed a technique for using automated matrix co-clustering to discover associations between customers and products.[4] The large volume of unstructured, social media data for LTS is an example of two of the 4 V's: *Volume* and *Variety*.[5] The LTS platform has been deployed worldwide and is being used by more than 1,000 sellers and practitioners in GTS. The assessments of existing opportunities from LTS help sellers determine which services opportunities are most likely to lead to sales, and the 360-degree views of companies, along with the product associations with customers, help sellers identify promising new business areas for services.

Outcome: Increased Signings, Revenue, and Pipeline

The impact of this platform's influence can be measured in millions of dollars in cost savings, millions of dollars in increased revenue, and billions of dollars in increased signings and pipeline.

Challenge: Predicting Risk of Contracts

A contract is an important element of a services business and needs to reflect the client's expectations. Further, if the terms of the contract can be met at the planned cost, the gross profit target for the contract will be met. However, if the contract has unforeseen risks that cause more resources to be used than planned or if IBM incurs penalties, the gross profit target will be missed. Unforeseen risks can also erode the quality of the client delivery. Accurately assessing the risks and mitigating those risks before signing a contact is imperative both for delivering excellent services to clients and for achieving the planned gross profit. A solution is needed to predict the risks of a new contract by comparing the contract characteristics to historical data of similar contracts. Chapter 4, "Anticipating the Financial Future," describes mergers and acquisitions analytics, which is used to predict which acquisitions are likely to succeed, based on historical data of previous acquisitions. GTS used a similar approach to predict which IT outsourcing contracts are likely to be successful. The solution for predicting contract risk, **Financial Risk Analytics**, leveraged learnings from the mergers and acquisitions solution.

Gross profit and risk predictions for a new contract are derived by aggregating historical results of similar contracts. The historical data associated with past contracts includes the "fingerprints" of the contract (key contract characteristics), observed gross profit delta, and reported root causes. For a new contract, Financial Risk Analytics predicts the total risk exposure to profit margin and the individual contract risks. Financial Risk Analytics also recommends mitigation actions for the risks.

Outcome: Deployment of Financial Risk Analytics

After strong results from prototyping, in March 2013, GTS operationally deployed Financial Risk Analytics to predict risk in its IT outsourcing contracts. To date, FRA has been used to assess more than 250 contracts. Given the life cycle of these contracts, it will be at least a year before broad-based impact can be measured.

Challenge: Optimizing Workforce Performance

Understanding and analyzing workforce performance is key to the success of IBM's services business and requires that information from multiple functions be integrated.

Daniel D'Elena, Vice President, IBM Global Business Services Worldwide Resource and Capacity Management, has been building capability in the area of workforce management for a number of years. Applying resources to client projects can be thought of as a manufacturing supply and demand problem. D'Elena and his team started by developing a view of the workforce (supply) and then moved to developing a view of client work (demand).

An early challenge that the team faced was that there were many inconsistent versions of the data across the organization. To address this challenge, they made the decision to develop tools to access centralized data. The first capability the team developed was an expertise taxonomy that includes job families, job roles, skill sets, and skills. The taxonomy is an important building block for managing supply and demand in GBS. Once you have a taxonomy with which to categorize skills, the next step is to get a view of supply. Dan established several tools to capture detailed views of the skills of employees. **Professional Development Tool** is a web-based application that allows employees to document their skills, allows managers to validate an employee's skills, and provides the data used to assess availability of skilled resources in IBM. The tool can also be used to identify skill gaps. **Professional Marketplace** is a tool for staffing. It is a source for demand for positions as well as availability of supply (skilled resources) to fill the positions. **CV Wizard** is an enterprise-wide application that allows employees to create and access curriculum vitae (CVs).

The next step is to get a view of demand—the expected business. GBS needed to capture demand at a detailed skill level since a services engagement generally requires very specialized skills. Developing a good staffing plan, which identifies the detailed skills and resources required for an opportunity, is an essential part of creating a low-risk contract. **Demand Capture** is a method to collect and maintain demand information and translate business opportunities from the sales channel into specific skill-based demand. As illustrated in Figure 10-2, Demand Capture takes the staffing plans and opportunities as input and matches available employees with the required skills from Professional Marketplace. The arrow from staffing plans to opportunities represents the resource planning that happens before the opportunity is closed. In the time period between closing the sale and beginning the work, some skill gaps can be closed, if needed. Demand Capture can also be used to alert GBS about shifts in the marketplace in real time.

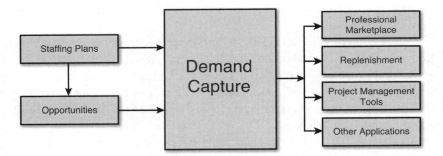

Figure 10-2 Demand Capture collects the skills demanded from staffing plans and matches resources from Professional Marketplace

GBS matched the demand and supply using analytics. In 2007, GBS created the first instance of the **Resource Analytics Hub**, an advanced analytics solution.[6] The Resource Analytics Hub resolves current staffing requirements, provides a visibility of future skill requirements, and optimizes resources. Further, the Resource Analytics Hub reduces the number of employees not assigned to client work (known as the "bench"), increases utilization of resources, and speeds up the capture of revenue. Figure 10-3 depicts the Resource Analytics Hub and the six facets that it integrates into a single view. The figure shows the groups and interactions of the groups. For each facet there is a different set of operations and leadership managers. Staffing managers, on the left of the figure, work in both demographics and availability. Similarly, capacity managers, on the right of the figure, work in both supply and demand. The resource managers make assignments on their own, but for availability, they support the staffing managers.

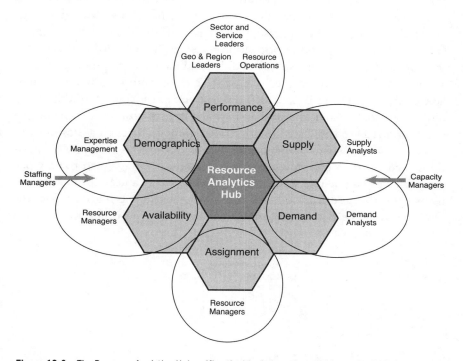

Figure 10-3 The Resource Analytics Hub unifies the big data and analytics needs of all services operations and leadership

In 2010, GTS created an instance of the Resources Analytics Hub to match supply and demand for strategic outsourcing.

The core of the Resource Analytics Hub is a flexible matching engine from IBM Research. It is important to note that resource-to-opening matching is not as simple as candidate identification because the goal is to fill as many openings as possible, making good matches. The matching engine, named **IBM Optimal Matching Technology (OMT)**, applies constraint programming, a discipline that draws from optimization and artificial intelligence.[7] OMT uses lists of available professionals, open positions, and a set of rules and prioritizations to determine near-optimal assignments that take into account all resources and positions in the pool, as well as complex constraints that define a good match. Work continues to refine and enhance the analytics capabilities of the Resource Analytics Hub.

Figure 10-4 illustrates the result of applying constraint programming to match people to positions. The assignment mode is comprised of two steps: prioritization and solving a constraint problem to determine a near-optimal assignment. Data about the open positions (demand) and data about the availability and skill of people (supply) are provided to the matching engine, OMT. Matching rules and prioritization rules are also provided to the matching engine. OMT uses the supply and demand data and the rules to produce a prioritization of five people, labeled 1, 2, 3, 4, and 5, to five positions, labeled A, B, C, D and E (see the rightmost box in the figure). In this example, three people match the skill and availability for position A. The people in the prioritization are listed in priority order for each position. Positions A, B, C, and D compete for the resources 1, 2, and 3. In this example, the positions occur in the same timeframe, so a person can be assigned to only one position. The engine uses a constraint solver to create a near-optimal assignment from the prioritization (see the lowest box in the figure, below the OMT). Given the constraints, only four of the five positions are matched with resources.

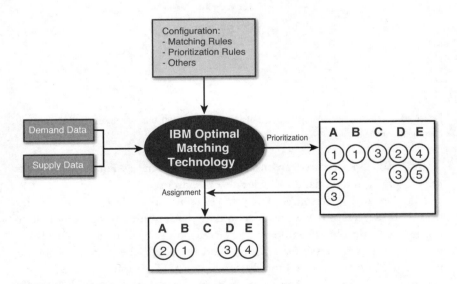

Figure 10-4   Using constraint programming to match people to positions

D'Elena learned several lessons on his journey to applying analytics to workforce planning and allocation. One is that sharing data across the organization is much better than allowing departments to hoard data and measurement is very important because you get what you inspect.

Outcome: Large Cost Savings, Improved Productivity, and Faster Client Response Times

In 2008, IBM was a Workforce Optimas Award winner in the category Financial Impact, in recognition of the Resource Analytics Hub that GBS created, which applies supply chain principles to workforce performance and has saved IBM more than $1 billion.[8]

GBS and GTS have achieved a number of positive outcomes through the use of the Resource Analytics Hub. GBS has improved productivity of consultants by 18% and reduced unassigned resources from 8% to 3%; both GBS and GTS have reduced their use of higher-cost subcontractors and have provided faster response times to clients by more rapidly finding the right resources.[9]

Challenge: Getting Early Warning About Problems

Successful services businesses drive client value profitably by delivering essential business capabilities to clients on time and at a planned cost. To meet these delivery objectives, services businesses deploy and utilize project portfolio delivery management systems and cadences to regularly qualify the health of services projects.

However, a services company may have thousands of projects in its portfolio to manage. Ensuring that the right projects in the portfolio get the right attention is critical. In addition to reduced client satisfaction and future growth opportunities, project risks that are not addressed in time through the portfolio management system may lead to troubled projects requiring additional, out-of-plan resources being applied in order to recover.

To meet this challenge, GBS has developed an analytics engine that leverages IBM Research-developed regression analysis–based predictive analytics indicators and project prioritization capabilities, project health data, and project financial data to provide an early-warning reporting system to the GBS business and service lines.[10] This analytics engine is part of the larger Analytics Framework that brings together data, analytics, and reporting, providing a complete solution for the business. Figure 10-5 illustrates the four components of the Analytics Framework: business performance data, an analytics engine, an analytics management system, and a delivery analytics dashboard. The data includes assessments; project review, financial, and health data; and customer satisfaction data. The analytics engine uses the data to predict future risks, based on patterns. The management system represents a single source of data for key business units. The dashboard is easy to use and has drill-downs for more detail and is the component most frequently used by GBS business and service-line leaders.

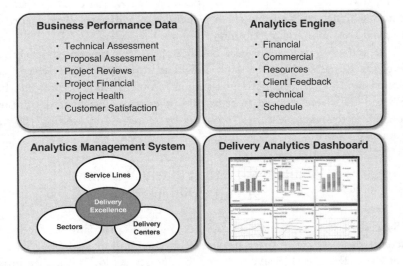

Figure 10-5   The GBS Analytics Framework, which drives delivery excellence

Outcome: Timely Intelligence to Delivery Teams to Help Satisfy Clients

According to Greg Dillon, Vice President, Global Delivery Excellence, IBM Global Business Services, "Our Analytics Framework allows us to gain visibility into the health of our project portfolio in a way we've never achieved in the past. We can deliver timely intelligence to our delivery teams across the globe and help them satisfy our clients."

Lessons Learned

Relationships inferred from data today may not be present in data collected tomorrow. Delivery excellence is a good example of this theme. A project can become troubled very quickly, even if the health of the project has been good for a number of months.

You don't have to understand analytics technology to derive value from it. The positive reception of the business and service-line leaders to the delivery analytics dashboard is an example of people making effective use of a tool without having a deep understanding of the analytics technology that provides the dashboard results.

It's important to leverage the levers. As discussed in Chapter 1, "Why Big Data and Analytics?" organizations that excel in leveraging the nine levers of differentiation derive the most value from data and analytics.[11] IBM Global Services has established a basis for data and analytics by taking actions and making decisions, which leverages the *Source of Value*; they *Measure* business outcomes; and the Long-Term Signings platform, Financial Risk Analytics, Resource Analytics Hub, and the Analytics Framework run on *Platforms* that allow people across Global Services to leverage them. IBM Global Services has established a *Culture* for the use of data and analytics, and it uses *Data* management practices.

Endnotes

1. "2013 Annual Report," Report of Financials, IBM Corporation. http://www.ibm.com/annualreport/2013/bin/assets/2013_ibm_financials.pdf.

2. Ibid.

3. Ibid.

4. Zouzias, A., Vlachos, M., and Freris, N., "Unsupervised Sparse Matrix Co-clustering for Marketing and Sales Intelligence," *Proceedings of the 16th Pacific-Asia Conference on Advances in Knowledge Discovery and Data Mining,* 2012. http://dl.acm.org/citation.cfm?id=2342644&CFID=281742076&CFTOKEN=43089809.

5. Schroeck, M., et al., "Analytics: The Real-World Use of Big Data—How Innovative Enterprises Extract Value from Uncertain Data," IBM Institute for Business Value, October 2012. http://www-03.ibm.com/systems/hu/resources/the_real_word_use_of_big_data.pdf.

6. Williams, R., "Strategic Work Force Planning: Best Practices from IBM Global Services," APQC, 2010.

7. Asaf, S., et al., "Applying Constraint Programming to Identification and Assignment of Service Professionals," *Lecture Notes in Computer Science,* Volume 6308, 2010. http://link.springer.com/chapter/10.1007%2F978-3-642-15396-9_5#page-1.

8. "2008 Optimas Awards Winners," *Workforce,* 2008. http://www.workforce.com/articles/2008-i-optimas-awards-i-winners.

9. Sanford, L., "The Road to a Smarter Enterprise: Six Principles to Consider," FWSIM CIO Executive Leadership Summit, October 25, 2010.

10. Ratakonda, K., et al., "Identifying Trouble Patterns in Complex IT Services Engagements," *IBM Journal of Research and Development*, Volume 54, Number 2, March/April 2010. http://ieeexplore.ieee.org/xpl/login. jsp?tp=&arnumber=5438939&url=http%3A%2F%2Fieeexplore.ieee. org%2Fiel5%2F5288520%2F5438932%2F05438939. pdf%3Farnumber%3D5438939.

11. Balboni, F., et al., "Analytics: A Blueprint for Value—Converting Big Data and Analytics Insights into Results," IBM Institute for Business Value, November 2013. http://public.dhe.ibm.com/common/ssi/ecm/ en/gbe03575usen/GBE03575USEN.PDF.

II

Reflections and a Look to the Future

"Study the past if you would define the future."

—Confucius

The Journey Continues

Analytics has been applied throughout IBM in organizations ranging from supply chain to finance to product development to human resources to sales, using techniques from a vast toolkit that includes descriptive statistics, predictive analytics, entity analytics, simulation, machine learning, and optimization. The chapters of this book describe 31 case studies, detailing the business challenges being faced, the data available, the methods applied, and the benefits realized. These stories also discuss the roles played by individuals in the definition, development, and deployment of analytics because, while computers may do the calculations necessary for analytics, people define the opportunities, identify the available data, and make use of the insights to inform decisions. Within IBM, analytics is very much a team effort. Although there are many individuals whose contributions, whether technical or managerial, were essential to the success of individual projects, it is safe to say that within IBM, the analytics journey has not been led by a single trailblazer. The progress has resulted from parallel efforts in multiple organizations; while each focused on its own specific business needs, data, tools, and expertise were shared. This sharing resulted in rapid improvements in data availability, understanding, and governance, as well as in the establishment of deployment patterns that engaged the right set of stakeholders for each project. The sharing also resulted in IBM being able to avoid many analytics pitfalls, as information about things that did not work was shared as widely as information about what did work.

- *Chapter 2, "Creating a Smarter Workforce":* The Workforce Analytics organization has decreased voluntary attrition in growth markets. They also took a bold step to develop a new social media solution based on a number of data sources, and the solution has provided much insight about what IBM employees think about various programs and topics. The organization learned that the value is not the *insight* but rather the *actions taken* as a result of the insight.

- *Chapter 3, "Optimizing the Supply Chain":* After working on a series of projects, the Smarter Supply Chain Analytics organization identified three critical success factors for realizing value through big data and analytics: The leadership from three teams (operations, process transformation, and analytics) must be ready for change, each of the three teams should have compelling business benefits, and starting small and working iteratively is the best approach.

- *Chapter 4, "Anticipating the Financial Future":* The Finance organization approached its transformation very pragmatically in order to move from reporting on the past to becoming a highly valued and trusted business advisor. In the process, Finance learned the importance of creating an analytics culture with strong executive support, clear targets, and measurable objectives.

- *Chapter 5, "Enabling Analytics Through Information Technology":* Big data and analytics are essential to the function of an IT organization. But even more importantly, the CIO organization is in an ideal position in an enterprise to enable transformation to leverage big data and analytics across the enterprise. The CIO organization has created several big data and analytics applications that are widely used; users get the benefits from the applications without knowing how the data and analytics make the applications work.

■ *Chapter 6, "Reaching Your Market":* Marketing leaders have an unprecedented opportunity to use analytics, big data, and social media to better
understand client needs, understand behaviors, and respond to those in
such a way that the client will have a "signature experience." IBM's
Marketing organization learned that doing something fast was better
than doing it perfectly. Through applied automation and analytics, marketing was able to increase by 14 times the response rate in one major
market while doubling the number of leads.

■ *Chapter 7: "Measuring the Immeasurable":* The Development ETI tackled
and measured what had previously been deemed "immeasurable," creating a new foundation for additional analytics. The team learned to use
analytics to fill gaps in the imperfect data and worked through many
organizational challenges with strong leadership and commitment.

■ *Chapter 8: "Optimizing Manufacturing":* IBM learned that fast, cheap
processors and cheap storage made possible analysis of the big data being
produced in its 300-mm fab. By analyzing the data, IBM was able to
improve chip yields, detect problems before they became problems, and
optimize performance across complex manufacturing processes.

■ *Chapter 9, "Increasing Sales Performance":* Improving sales effectiveness
directly impacts the bottom line, and IBM's Sales organization has taken
a highly proactive approach to leveraging big data and analytics to do
just that. Users of the recommendations from the analytics models derive
business value without needing to understand the algorithms and inner
workings of the model.

■ *Chapter 10, "Delivering Services with Excellence":* IBM Global Services is
realizing benefits from data and analytics in multiple areas of the business, including identifying top pursuits, predicting contract risk, enhancing workforce performance, and predicting client project performance.

Reflections

As the writing of this book concludes in early 2014, the use of analytics
within IBM continues to grow. Teams in IBM Research continue to expand
the set of addressable analytics problems through advances in hardware,
information storage and access, and algorithms. Much of the emphasis is on
the use of parallel computation on distributed data, with the goal being creation of deep insights based on aggregated data on the fly, without the physical aggregation of the data. Additional work is under way to make

analytics-based results more accessible and understandable to end users and to make those results available in the context of the user's role, providing recommendations, as needed, in a role-based workflow. Areas not discussed in this book, such as Real Estate Planning and Facility Management for IBM's worldwide office, lab, and manufacturing space, as well as Intellectual Property Licensing, are also deploying analytics to improve their business performance. IBM also provides analytics software and services to thousands of clients, with a growing portfolio of offerings that includes both tools for the analytically skilled to build applications and complete applications that address specific business processes. IBM established a global community called AnalyticsZone to help enable others on their analytic journey through downloads, tools, and more.

As IBM undertook the development and deployment of analytics within its own business functions, the scarcity of skills became apparent. IBM was fortunate to have an extensive pool of expertise in the disciplines underlying analytics in the Research division, along with information technology and business skills distributed throughout the company. In addition, IBM employees who used analytics formed a practitioners' community that shared information and knowledge through seminars, forums, and information repositories. When business function teams, such as Human Resources and Finance, needed to increase their skills in analytics, material from the practitioners' community and other internal training material was readily available. In 2013, Emily Plachy and Maureen Norton launched the Analytic Ambassador community. Ambassadors advocate the use of analytics, give talks about big data and analytics topics, and mentor others to increase the number of skilled resources within IBM, thereby widening the ripple effect of influence and impact.

While IBM's internal analytics capability could be shared across business units and expanded through internal training at a rate sufficient to meet internal needs, the capacity of IBM's clients' other enterprises to make effective use of analytics was a concern. Clients repeatedly asked IBM for help in establishing analytics teams, in recruiting skills, and in updating the skills of their current staff. IBM's University Relations team has more than 1,000 partnerships with universities and colleges around the world to establish a range of analytics programs at both the undergraduate and graduate level. Most prevalent are master's degree programs in analytics, offered by either business schools or engineering schools. While some schools have chosen to offer complete degree programs in analytics, others have added an analytics concentration to existing master's programs or have created certificate programs intended primarily for midcareer business or information technology employees. Applications to all these programs are high, as are job opportunities for the graduates. IBM provides free access to many analytics software products, course materials, and guest lecturers for these programs, along with mini-conferences for the faculty at IBM's annual analytics users' conference. This book can be used within these programs, and supporting teaching materials will be made available to faculty.

With clear evidence of business value and a growing population of skilled users, it is interesting to consider what the future holds for analytics. For this discussion, *analytics* is defined broadly as the use of data and computation to make informed decisions. Analytics can clearly be used simply to gain insight; however, the value is realized when that insight informs a decision and then an action that would otherwise not have been taken is made. Ideally, that action results in a better outcome than would otherwise have occurred, and, in most cases, that action should be taken with at least an expectation of a better outcome. However, there can be long-term benefit from taking an action that results only in better information, not in a better outcome, if that information is remembered and used to inform future decisions.

Transactional Data

Transactional data, the data produced by the IT systems that run a business, remains a huge source of untapped data for analytics. Many enterprises use the data about what has happened only to create reports. The opportunity to use the data to make predictions about what will happen and to understand the decision levers available to influence what will happen remains underexploited. Applying statistical and data mining methods to transactional data is fairly easy. Coupled with data visualization and exploration methods, these methods can be used to gain far greater understanding of how a business or business process works—what underlying trends exist, which outcomes are correlated, and, most importantly, which actions are most likely to produce specific outcomes. It is important to note that while some of the relationships present in transactional data may result from the physical or business logic embedded in the business process and hence in the automation supporting it, other relationships may have no physical or business explanation. For example, "for each car manufactured, five tires are required" is a result of the bill-of-materials for a car specifying four tires (or five, for cars that still come with a spare) while "for every ten cars ordered, four are ordered in silver and two are ordered in black" is simply a reflection of the current color preferences of buyers for that make and model of car. However, as long as the second relationship remains true, it is just as useful in planning purchases and scheduling the manufacturing facilities as the first relation-ship. In analytics, distinguishing between relationships that are always true is important, typically because they represent physical or business relation-ships, as opposed to those that simply appear to be true from the available data. Relationships of the former type can be used with confidence in all decision making. Relationships of the latter type must be used with care and should be retested often. In fact, the realization that relationships of the second type could be used at all for many practitioners marks the sudden increase in the potential for the field of analytics.

Simulation

Simulation can also be used along with transactional data. Simulation models are typically built based on experts' views on how the parts of a com-plicated system work. Chapter 5 discusses an application for deciding when to modernize servers that uses Monte Carlo simulation and predictive model-ing. Transactional data that describes how a system worked in the past can be used to validate a simulation model. In addition, it can be used to character-ize the variability of key factors (for example, product demand, manufactur-ing tool failure rates) that are used to describe the external factors needed to simulate the future. However, to be truly useful for decision making, simula-tions need to represent how the business could behave in the future, starting from the current state, considering a range of external scenarios and many sets of internal decisions. These possible future paths then become additional data to be explored, analyzed, and visualized. Simulation has been used to study supply chains and evaluate everything from location of factories to transportation policies. It has been used to study epidemics and evaluate pol-icy decisions such as the closing of schools and distribution of vaccines. Simulation is commonly used in the financial industry to compute the possi-ble future value of investments under different economic scenarios and inher-ent market fluctuations, and thus, estimate the value at risk in a portfolio. Outside the financial industry, simulation is currently underutilized in ana-lytics, in part because of the difficulty of creating and maintaining the simu-lation models and keeping them aligned with the current state of the system being studied. But only through computing and aggregating a representative set of possible future outcomes is it possible to translate uncertainty into risk and then make risk-informed decisions. As more data accumulates, as more simulation modeling skills become available, and as decision makers become more accustomed to dealing with representations of uncertainty, simulation is likely to be applied more broadly to support decision making.

Simulation, through repeated runs representing different scenarios or different realizations of variability, naturally produces a set of outcomes—one for each run. Applying statistical analysis to these outcomes enables the generation of confidence intervals—that is, a range in which the actual outcome will lie with a specified probability, typically 95%. Other predictive analysis techniques also lend themselves to the calculation of confidence intervals or other certainty measures. However, end users have shown a strong preference for dealing with simple, single-point answers rather than confidence intervals or distributions. The ability to reason with and make decisions based on intervals, distributions, or other complex representations of possible choices is being addressed in some of the analytics education offered at universities. Therefore, whenever possible, analytics methods and applications should be able to provide more detailed explanations of options and possible outcomes, while still enabling the user to identify simple recommendations or signals from within the data. One interesting use of confidence measures was exhibited in the *Jeopardy!* match between the Watson computer and two human champions. For each possible answer Watson found, it also computed its confidence that the answer was correct and used that confidence value to determine whether to venture an answer and how much to wager in Final *Jeopardy!*

Alerts

A first step in moving from batch-oriented, descriptive analytics to near real-time use of predictive analytics is the use of alerts. In the simplest form, an alert simply notifies an end user when a computed value is outside a pre-specified range. For example, individuals use alerts offered by their banks to notify them when an account balance drops below a certain level. An alert provides an early warning of an undesirable event, such as a bounced check, by determining a safety margin, such as the balance level that would be crossed some time before the undesirable event occurred, giving the recipient of the alert time to take action. A predictive method that produces confidence intervals can be used to construct an alert that will inform the user whenever the probability of the undesirable event exceeds a specified threshold. Predictive alerting methods that take into account not only the current state but historical data, correlations between different measured values, and even the possibility of taking mitigating action are likely to become available for a wide range of applications. An emerging area involves predictive maintenance of heavy equipment. This approach uses data from a host of sensors on the equipment and aggregates usage, failure, and repair data across many pieces of equipment to estimate the probability of failure within a certain time window and to recommend alternate usage modes, as well as preventive maintenance.

Forecasting

IBM has used forecasting for several decades to predict weekly or monthly product sales. The product sales forecast is used as an input to both manufacturing planning and financial planning. As described in Chapter 4, IBM's Finance organization uses forecasting methods to predict revenue at both local and global aggregations. Forecasting methods can also be used to predict organizational spending in specific categories, such as payroll, travel, and benefits-related expenses. IBM also uses forecasting methods to determine the inventory and labor required for its hardware maintenance business, and it couples this forecasting with optimization methods that recommend where to position the inventory, given the location of the computers under contract.

Forecasting for high-volume products is well studied and readily addressed, along with pricing, by a number of commercial software packages, including IBM's DemandTec®. In contrast, forecasting for very low volumes or, similarly, for rare events, is less well studied and is a subject of current research. A good example of low-volume part failure and forecasting is the statistically based field of reliability engineering, which originated in the aerospace industry and NASA. Forecasting for very low-volume maintenance parts amounts to estimating the probability that a part will be needed to service a failure in a specified amount of time and thus is equivalent to forecasting when different types of (rare) failure events will occur.

An additional area of active investigation in demand forecasting involves searching for correlations between time series, such as time series representing weekly demand for different products. When there are correlations accompanied by time offsets, one time series can be used as an early signal for the other time series. That is, the actual current and recent past values for demand for one product are used to predict the future demand of a different product. Finding such pairs is computationally intense, potentially requiring computing the correlation between every pair of items at every reasonable offset. Finding triples in which a pair of items is predictive of a third item requires potentially examining every threesome of items, and the computational requirements expand as larger sets are considered. Even with the computing power we expect to have available in the near future, brute-force computational approaches will not be practical. Filtering methods that eliminate many possible combinations from consideration or identify a small number of combinations for examination with minimal computation are needed to make such approaches reasonable. In addition to considering correlation between demand for one product and demand for another product, identifying correlation between product demand and other time series can be valuable in producing accurate forecasts. Advertising placement, product announcements, competitors' product announcements, and seller contact can all be represented as time series and correlated against product sales. Perhaps most interestingly, buyer and influencer sentiment can also be extracted from text in technical literature and on buyer community websites, and this sentiment, which may change over time both in tone and in volume, can be correlated with sales data to sometimes identify additional sources of demand prediction data.

As the many examples in this book show, analyzing data to find trends and signals that predict some future outcome is often possible. Most of the methods used involve considering large sets of data for which the outcome of interest is already known. In addition to the known outcome, each data point includes multiple features representing known facts about the item of interest. A goal of predictive analytics is to understand whether and how different features are correlated with different outcomes. Ideally, the analysis produces a scoring model that can be applied to a new collection of features for which the outcome is not yet known. The scoring model may either compute the most likely outcome or the probability of each of the possible outcomes. Many methods are available to create predictive models. Most of the projects in IBM have used methods that are available in the IBM SPSS product set. For these projects, the data sets have been large—but not so large as to require that the data and computation be distributed. Generally, data scientists used their knowledge of the data and of the business process to extract tens or hundreds of features, but not tens of thousands of features. In most cases, the number of data points examined at IBM has been in the thousands to hundreds of thousands, or it could be a subset of this size without concern for loss of information.

The Future

"Nothing in the world is so powerful as an idea whose time has come."

—Victor Hugo

Several dynamics are underway that are shaping the future for big data and analytics.[1] The amount of data being generated is huge—2.5 billion gigabytes every day, most of which is unstructured such as social media, video, audio, images, and data from sensors. The large volume of data will make it difficult to gain insight from data in time to act. Fortunately, cognitive systems will enable us to rapidly explore big data and uncover insights.

Growth of Data

As businesses continue to operate, the body of transactional data grows. As additional functions are automated and additional information is collected, the amount of data in a transaction may also grow. Thus, the repository of transactional data within an enterprise is potentially growing at a more than linear rate. Predictive modeling methods are being redesigned to deal with the increase in both the depth (number of data elements) and width (number of features) of data sets. Currently the data sets generated by the semiconductor manufacturing lines are among the largest routinely mined for insight within IBM. (Chapter 8 described how this data is used to improve yields and quality.) However, as data processing centers themselves are instrumented, and as computing is increasingly performed in large shared clouds, the log data being generated by the computational processes is rapidly growing. Examination of this data to predict device or process failures, to estimate task completion time, and to better allocate work and data across the available resources will increasingly become a focus of data scientists and analytics professionals. The Internet of Things—the embedding of objects with sensors coupled with the ability of objects to communicate—is driving an explosion in the growth of big data. This data will also increasingly become a focus of data scientists and analytics professionals.

Mathematical optimization, an analytics technique used in many of the examples in this book, is applicable when there are causal relationships or correlation between actions and outcomes or between sets of actions. Linear programming and integer programming, two commonly used mathematical optimization techniques, are available in the IBM ILOG CPLEX product and have been applied to logistics and manufacturing problems where actions and outcomes are linked by the physical processes involved. Over the past decade, optimization methods have also been applied in instances where some of the relationships linking actions and outcomes are inferred from the data through the use of statistics or mining techniques. As previously discussed, the inferred relationships must be continually tested and refreshed as new data becomes available. However, with this limitation addressed by solutions that combine a mining step with an optimization step, optimization can be used to get the most out of marketing spending, to allocate skilled resources to projects, to manage complex product development processes, and for a host of other resource allocation problems that arise within IBM. CPLEX and other similar products require that the relationship be deterministic, meaning that they typically cannot directly deal with variability or uncertainty. Coupling optimization with simulation or other means of capturing variability is an area of active research in IBM.

As business processes become automated, the associated decision processes also need to be automated. This is currently accomplished primarily through the use of business rules that capture existing business decision logic. Predictive and prescriptive methods, such as optimization, can be used to create rules by codifying previous decisions captured in past transaction data. They can also be used to improve rules by selecting only those actions that resulted in favorable outcomes. It is also possible to directly use optimization methods to generate automated business decisions, although the computational cost of running the optimization code must be justified by the resulting improved outcomes. A hybrid approach, in which rules are used to execute decisions in near real time while optimization runs in the background and periodically adjusts the rules, is likely to be necessary for some classes of resource allocation problems, particularly those that arise in managing the operation of large data centers or computing clouds.

Unstructured Data

A number of the analytics projects discussed in this book have used structured data from IBM's internal business automation systems. One exception is the Enterprise Social Pulse work described in Chapter 2, which has used free-text data as input and has created an analysis of employee sentiment. Several sales examples in Chapter 9 use external structured data—for example, Dun & Bradstreet. The Crunch Day example from Chapter 6 used external unstructured data from Twitter. In addition, some of the projects have used free-text fields within structured data sets, with some "cleansing" of the free text required to generate valid categorical data. Generations of statisticians and computer scientists have studied structured data, and extensive capability has been developed to store, compress, extract, query, summarize, analyze, and visualize structured data. Other forms of digitized data— notably text data, audio data, image data, and video data—are now being stored and analyzed in thousands of loosely connected exercises around the world. The term *unstructured data* is used to refer to information (typically stored digitally) that either does not have a predefined data model or is not organized in a predefined manner. Most unstructured data is text created by humans. It includes emails, documents, text messages, tweets, status updates on social media sites, reviews on product sites, blogs, and more. Unstructured data may include numbers such as prices or dates, but the data is typically not labeled as such. While structured data is relatively easy for a computer to act on, as the data model specifies how each type of data should be dealt with, unstructured data is difficult to process using traditional computer programs.

Most of the unstructured internal IBM data is text data, including invention disclosures, product literature, project documents, personnel records, client proposals and contracts, business plans, and press releases. Understanding the content of text documents is commonly referred to as *content analytics*. Within IBM, the Unstructured Information Management Architecture (UIMA)[2] is used as a framework for natural language processing of text documents.

One use of unstructured data within IBM involves constructing relationship graphs that show linkages between employees. These linkages are derived from text documents. For example, the "from" and "to" fields of an email imply a relationship between the sender and the recipient, and the subject of an email or its contents may describe the type or context of the relationship. Co-authorship of a report or patent application implies a relationship between the authors that is related to the topic of the report or patent. Understanding the correlation between the size, structure, and participants in a network and specific business outcomes would be of potential value within IBM, as patterns that are correlated with favorable outcomes could be encouraged, while management attention could be applied to intercept and redirect patterns that are correlated with negative outcomes.

IBM provides many self-service learning opportunities to its employees, utilizing recorded webcasts, documents, and online short courses. Educational content is accessed through the corporate intranet, and thus it is possible to keep track of when each employee accesses each piece of content. In addition to collecting direct and immediate feedback from employees regarding their perception of the usefulness of content, certain business outcomes can be analyzed against training data to determine the business value of the educational content. Such analysis would have to be at a very granular level, considering the job role and previous knowledge of the employee. Ultimately, such analysis could also be used proactively, to suggest specific content to individual employees to help them make best use of their time.

IBM, like many other enterprises, uses social computing to facilitate collaboration and information sharing among employees and to replace traditional "push-down" communication with the social computing processes of status updates, blogs, and following of individuals or topics. However, social computing within IBM isn't merely about being social; it is about shortening communication paths, engaging employees, and better serving clients. The *client collaboration hubs* (*CCHs*) use social computing to achieve these goals. For each of IBM's large clients, a CCH, moderated by the IBM executives responsible for that client, provides a place where information about the client's business and details on IBM's interactions with that client can be found. The CCH facilitates knowledge sharing and collaboration among the IBM teams that serve a client. IBM teams also use the hubs to construct responses to request for proposals and to prepare for client meetings. The hubs have reduced the need for phone calls and emails and have enabled IBM teams to more effectively address clients' needs. Additional hubs are being created for teams that serve collections of smaller clients. While these hubs are expected to immediately improve IBM's productivity, as their use increases and as content within them expands, they may become data sources for new analytics. Examining data from many hubs and many activities (for example, meetings, proposal preparations), incorporating corresponding transactional data, and searching for patterns that correlate with specific types of outcomes may lead to identification of best practices as well as the creation of early warning signals. As with any other use of analytics, sufficient data must be accumulated before patterns can be found. As social computing is used in additional IBM business processes, the information artifacts such as text (for example, blogs, queries, comments), counts (for example, views, reposts, "likes"), and links (for example, person-to-person, person-to-account, person-to-skill) that accumulate will provide additional opportunities for the application of analytics.

Cognitive Computing

The triumph of the Watson computer over two human champions in the quiz show *Jeopardy!* marked the beginning of a new era of computing. The first era of computing, the tabulating era, was characterized by special-purpose machines used to address the burdensome tasks of counting, sorting, and recording. The second era of computing, the programmable systems era, was characterized by general-purpose machines that are programmed by humans to perform a wide range of computational tasks. The third era, the cognitive era, is characterized by computing systems that are sensing, learning, reasoning, and interacting with people in new ways to provide insight and advice.[3] Cognitive computing promises to provide invaluable assistance with the analysis of big data. Examples include visualizing big data insights based on our questions, helping us explore data and uncover insights, and helping us detect anomalies in big data. While all but one of the analytics applications presented in this book make use of traditional programming methods, IBM has already begun to use the Watson cognitive technology internally.

Watson Sales Assistant, described in Chapter 5, is an internal pilot of IBM Watson to help IBM sellers answer questions about IBM products and offerings for their clients. It is based on the Watson platform and has been extended with IBM-specific content, dictionaries, ontology, and analytics. The internal beta version of the tool is being rolled out as this book is being written. As with other analytics projects, it is expected that the internal learnings will influence IBM's cognitive computing offerings. In addition, as the IBM Watson group uses cognitive computing to address a broad class of decision processes and transform other industries, the new capabilities will be applied across IBM in projects that have yet to be imagined.

IBM's journey in the use of analytics across the enterprise is far from over. Many of the examples shared in this book are just beginning to tap into the vast potential that this time in history offers. IBM's transformation will continue as additional capabilities from IBM Research in cognitive computing methods are leveraged in new and innovative ways. The lessons learned from these real-world applications of big data and analytics are shared here with the intent to spark an "aha" reaction in leaders and students alike and illuminate new possibilities. Innovation and growth will belong to enterprises that invest in becoming smarter. Where will your journey take you?

Endnotes

1. "2013 Annual Report, Chairman's Letter," IBM Corporation. http://www.ibm.com/annualreport/2013/chairmans-letter.html.
2. Apache UIMA, http://uima.apache.org.
3. Kelly, J. E., and Hamm, S. *Smart Machines: IBM's Watson and the Era of Cognitive Computing*, Columbia Business School Publishing, 2013. http://cup.columbia.edu/static/cognitive.

A

Big Data and Analytics Use Cases

Use Case	Business Challenge	Business Outcome	Chapter	Additional Uses	Types of Data	Analytics Techniques
Accounts receivable	Improving the accounts receivable business process and collector productivity	Better visibility to track total receivables view across entire collection process, labor cost reduction	3, "Optimizing the Supply Chain"	Accounts receivable	Historical payment data	Predictive analytics, optimization, business rules
Business case	Creating a smarter commerce B2B solution to drive cross-company efficiencies	An analytics-based, client-focused business case wins approval	9, "Increasing Sales Performance"	Approach can be used when building business case	Big data (*Volume*), profitability data from COP, revenue, growth rates, wallet share percentage	Predictive analytics
Business development	Developing new business	Increased sign-ings, revenue, and pipeline	10, "Delivering Services with Excellence"	Any new business development	Big data (*Volume* and *Variety*); social media data (IBM Connections, LinkedIn); structured data (financial databases)	Entity analytics, text analytics, predictive analytics
Detecting problems	Detecting quality problems early	Significant cost savings, improved productivity, improved brand value	3, "Optimizing the Supply Chain"	Manufacturing: detecting quality problems with product manufacturing	Big data (*Volume* and *Velocity*); parametric data from many thousand sources	Cumulative sum (CSUM), alerts

Use Case	Business Challenge	Business Outcome	Chapter	Additional Uses	Types of Data	Analytics Techniques
Detecting problems	Reducing the time to detect aberrant events	Engineers take action	8, "Optimizing Manufacturing"	Any manufacturing business	Big data (*Volume*); process trace data: hundreds of chemical, physical, and mechanical sensors that collect data while wafers are being processed	Univariate analysis, mean and variance of time-series data, scoring
Detecting problems	Getting early warning about problems	Timely intelligence to delivery teams to help satisfy clients	10, "Delivering Services with Excellence"	Most complex projects	Assessment data, financials, project health, customer satisfaction	Regression analysis, predictive analytics
Forecasting spending	Improving operational efficiency and effectiveness of managing worldwide spending	More efficient and effective spend forecasting	4, "Anticipating the Financial Future"	Sales, manufacturing	Sales data, ledger	Predictive analytics
Foundational	Getting the basics in place	Provided a single-view, common set of data to work from	4, "Anticipating the Financial Future" (See "Perspective" section.)	Additional analytics projects across the enterprise	Ledger, transactional systems	Predictive analytics

Use Case	Business Challenge	Business Outcome	Chapter	Additional Uses	Types of Data	Analytics Techniques
Foundational	Creating an analytics culture	Significant high-level support and innovative programs drive culture change	4, "Anticipating the Financial Future" (See "Perspective" section.)	All areas of the business	Varied	N/A
Foundational	Developing the data foundation and analytics capability to enable a signature client experience	Individual data master records to provide client-level insights	6, "Reaching Your Market"	The individual data master can be used across the enterprise	Client purchase history, company profile data	Predictive analytics
Foundational	Creating a common view of development expense to enable decision making	Development Expense Baseline project proves that the immeasurable can be measured	7, "Measuring the Immeasurable"	N/A	Data from finance, accounting, and HR	Text mining, nearest-neighbor algorithm, business rules, predictive analytics
Generating passion	Tapping into analytics passion to provide new insights to inform IBM's digital strategy	Insights from diverse teams provided the evidence needed to make changes to the digital strategy	6, "Reaching Your Market"	Any organization or school	Tweets from Twitter	Social media analytics, text analytics, sentiment analysis

Use Case	Business Challenge	Business Outcome	Chapter	Additional Uses	Types of Data	Analytics Techniques
Improving yield	Enhancing yield in the manufacturing of semiconductors	Cost savings due to yield improvement	8, "Optimizing Manufacturing"	Any manufacturing business	Big data (*Volume* and *Velocity*); process trace data: hundreds of chemical, physical, and mechanical sensors that collect data while wafers are being processed, sometimes in near real time	Data mining
Managing inventory	Providing supply/demand visibility and improved channel inventory management	Reduced price protection expense, reduced returns	3, "Optimizing the Supply Chain"	N/A	Big data (*Volume*); data feeds from downstream signals	Inventory/cost trade-off model, optimization, forecasting
Managing IT	Deciding when to modernize servers	Increase in application availability	5, "Enabling Analytics Through Information Technology"	N/A	Incident tickets for servers	Random forest model, Monte Carlo simulation, predictive modeling

Use Case	Business Challenge	Business Outcome	Chapter	Additional Uses	Types of Data	Analytics Techniques
Managing: IT	Detecting security incidents	Increased detection of security incidents	5, "Enabling Analytics Through Information Technology"	N/A	Big data (*Volume* and *Velocity*); many data sources integrated and parsed in real time	Rules to detect security anomalies
Marketing effectiveness	Going beyond correlation to determine causal effects of marketing actions	System deals with special terms and conditions added; grew from 67% to 98% over three quarters	6, "Reaching Your Market"	Select cases where correlation is insufficient to take the next action, can be used to determine causal effects	Historical data, 3,300 contracts for 1,200 clients over a 6-year period; revenue data	Observational study
Marketing effectiveness	Providing a real-time view into effectiveness of marketing actions: performance management	Marketing efficiencies realized and transformation of marketing enabled	6, "Reaching Your Market"	Internal approach commercialized for use by other enterprises	Open rates, click-through rates, campaign metrics	Enterprise market management automation
Predicting disruptions	Predicting disruptions in the supply chain	Number of listening events increased tenfold; local language listing proved valuable	3, "Optimizing the Supply Chain"	Marketing: market intelligence	Big data (*Variety*, *Volume*, and *Velocity*); social media (blogs, forums, boards, reviews, videos, online, Twitter, Facebook, LinkedIn, and news feeds	Social media analytics, text analytics, sentiment analysis

Use Case	Business Challenge	Business Outcome	Chapter	Additional Uses	Types of Data	Analytics Techniques
Predicting global tax	Improving productivity and accuracy while minimizing risk in tax and statutory reporting	Improved statutory and tax reporting, commercial product based on internal use and analytics	4, "Anticipating the Financial Future"	All companies that have global tax and compliance needs	Tax codes, regulations	Predictive analytics, text analytics
Predicting risk	Balancing risk and reward	Country Financial Risk Scorecard uses big data to monitor trends and minimize risk	4, "Anticipating the Financial Future"	All areas of the business with local presence in countries	Big data, financial data, economic reports	Predictive analytics, regression analysis
Predicting risk	Validating acquisition strategy	Mergers and Acquisitions improves success rate	4, "Anticipating the Financial Future"	Business areas that incorporate the acquired companies, mergers and acquisitions companies	Historical performance data on acquisitions, company information	Predictive analytics
Predicting risk	Predicting risk of contracts	Deployment of financial risk analytics	10, "Delivering Services with Excellence"	Predicting risk with a contract	Historical contract data, financial data	Predictive analytics
Product portfolio simplification	Simplifying the hardware product portfolio	Significant reduction of hardware product portfolio	8, "Optimizing Manufacturing"	Any product business	Data integration challenges	Predictive analytics

Use Case	Business Challenge	Business Outcome	Chapter	Additional Uses	Types of Data	Analytics Techniques
Revenue growth	Deploying sellers for maximum revenue growth by account	Increased sales performance	9, "Increasing Sales Performance"	Other sales organizations	Big data, territory revenue, number of clients, geographic location	Optimization
Revenue growth	Deploying sellers within a territory	Increased territory performance	9, "Increasing Sales Performance"	Other sales organizations	Market opportunity, client segmentation, industry categorization	Optimization
Revenue growth	Determining optimal sales coverage investment by account	Increased revenue and productivity	9, "Increasing Sales Performance"	Managing and distributing human resources	Big data (for example, revenue, seller activity, client opportunity)	Optimization
Scheduling manufacturing	Scheduling a complex manufacturing process in a semiconductor fab	Reduced production times	8, "Optimizing Manufacturing"	Any manufacturing business	Manufacturing processes, tool processing rates, work loads	Integer programming; constraint programming; business rules
Sentiment analysis	Gaining an accurate view of what employees are thinking	Ability to act on real insights about employees	2, "Creating a Smarter Workforce"	Marketing: customer views on products	Big data (*Variety*, *Volume*, and *Velocity*); social media (IBM Connections, Twitter, Facebook, LinkedIn)	Social media analytics, text analytics, sentiment analysis

Use Case	Business Challenge	Business Outcome	Chapter	Additional Uses	Types of Data	Analytics Techniques
Workforce optimization	Optimizing workforce performance	Large cost savings, improved productivity, faster client response times	10, "Delivering Services with Excellence"	Workforce management	Staffing plans, opportunity data, demographics, skill data	Optimization (constraint programming)
Workforce retention	Retaining high-value resources in growth markets	Attrition rate declined; net benefits exceeded expectations	2, "Creating a Smarter Workforce"	Workforce management	Historical employee data	Predictive analytics, clustering

Glossary: Acronyms and Definitions of Key Big Data and Analytics Terms

A

ACE   Analytics Center of Excellence

AER   Accelerated External Reporting

Alerts   Notifications to one or more end users that occur when a computed value is outside a prespecified range.

AQ   Analytics Quotient

B

B2B   Business–to-business

B2C   Business-to-consumer

BI   Business intelligence

Big data   The term that refers to data that has one or more of the following dimensions, known as the four *V*s: *Volume*, *Variety*, *Velocity*, and *Veracity*.

Business intelligence   The practice of reporting what has happened, analyzing contributing data to determine why it happened, and monitoring new data to determine what is happening now. It may include data summarization, visualization, and data interactions capability. Also known as *descriptive analytics* and *reporting*.

Business rule   A rule that captures business decision logic.

C

CCH   Client Collaboration Hub

CEO   Chief Executive Officer

CFO   Chief Financial Officer

CIO   Chief Information Officer

Clustering   The practice of grouping a set of data so that data within each cluster is similar and data from different clusters is not similar.

CMO   Chief Marketing Officer

Cognitive computing   A new form of computing, characterized by computing systems that sense, learn, reason, and interact with people to provide insight and advice.

Constraint programming   Programming in which relations between variables are expressed as constraints or restrictions.

COP   Coverage Optimization with Profitability

CRISP-DM   Cross-Industry Standard Process for Data Mining

CRM   Customer relationship management

Crunch Day   A 24-hour analytics event during which teams compete, have fun, and develop fresh insights by analyzing a collection of data.

CTO   Chief Technology Officer

Cube   A set of data organized by dimensions and measures for the purpose of aggregating different subsets of the larger set of data.

CUSUM   Cumulative Sum

CXO   Chief X Officer, where X is a function such as "Executive," "Marketing," "Information," or "Financial."

D

Data mart   Data organized to support specific needs of a user community.

Data mining   The practice of analyzing big data using mathematical models to develop insights, usually including machine learning algorithms as opposed to statistical methods.

Data warehouse   A store that provides data from the originating source or the operational data stores; it contains historical and derived data. Also known as an *information warehouse.*

Descriptive analytics   The practice of reporting what has happened, analyzing contributing data to determine why it happened, and monitoring new data to determine what is happening now. Also known as *reporting* and *business intelligence.*

E

EMM   Enterprise marketing management

Engagement analytics   The practice of analyzing systems of engagement to determine their effectiveness in areas such as activity, reaction, eminence, and network.

Enterprise market management automation   The process of automating marketing processes such as next-best-action and campaign management that otherwise would have been performed manually or would not have been possible.

Entity analytics   The practice of sorting through data and discovering data that relates to the same entity.

ETI   Enterprise Transformation Initiative

F

FLAG   Financial Leadership Advocacy Group

Forecasting   The practice of predicting or estimating a future event or trend, typically from historical data.

Four *Vs*   The four dimensions of big data: *Volume*, *Variety*, *Velocity*, and *Veracity.*

FPO   Fab PowerOps

G

GAAP   Generally accepted accounting principles

GBS   Global Business Services

GIE   Globally integrated enterprise

GTS   Global Technology Services

H

HPMT   Hardware Product Management Transformation

I

iBAT   IBM Buy Analysis Tool

IBM   International Business Machines

IFRS   International Finance Reporting Standards

Information delivery front end   A user interface that provides data for reporting and dashboard needs.

Information warehouse   *See* Data warehouse.

Integer programming   A mathematical optimization problem with binary unknowns.

Internet of Things   The embedding of objects with sensors, coupled with the ability of objects to communicate, driving an explosion in the growth of big data.

Inventory cost tradeoff model   A model in which price protection terms are changed to incentivize partners to maintain inventory based on the weekly replenishment model. The goal is to optimize inventory while maintaining serviceability under variable demand.

ISC   Integrated supply chain

J

Jeopardy!   An American television quiz show created by Merv Griffin in which contestants compete to provide correct questions to answers. *See* http://www.jeopardy.com.

L

LTS   Long-term signings

M

M&A   Mergers and Acquisitions

M&C   Marketing and Communications

MAP   Market Alignment Program

Markov decision process   A framework for modeling decision making.

Master data   Data that is key to the operation of a business, such as data about customers, suppliers, partners, products, and materials.

Master data stores   Data stores for master data.

MDP   Markov decision process

Monte Carlo simulation   Simulation that relies on random sampling.

N

Nearest neighbor algorithm   A method used for classification and regression. Cases are analyzed, and class membership is assigned based on similarity to other cases, where cases that are similar (or "near" in characteristics) are known as neighbors.

O

OMT   Optimal Matching Technology

Operational data store   A data store that provides data from the original source in near real time.

Optimization   Analysis techniques such as linear programming and integer programming that solve for multiple decision variables coupled with multiple constraints simultaneously. Generally used to recommend actions. *See also* Prescriptive analytics.

P

PMQ   Predictive Maintenance and Quality

Predictive analytics   The practice of using statistics and data mining to analyze current and historical information to make predictions about what will happen in the future. Predictive modeling, the fitting of some data to some model, is a step in predictive analytics. Typically, predictive analytics also includes applying a model to additional data.

Predictive modeling   A step in predictive analytics that involves fitting some data to some model. *See* Predictive analytics.

Prescriptive analytics   The analytics methods that recommend actions with the goal of finding a set of action that is predicted to produce the best possible outcome. *See also* Optimization.

Q

QEWS   Quality Early Warning System

R

Random forest model   A nonlinear statistical learning method.

Regression analysis   A statistical technique for estimating relationships between variables.

Reporting   The practice of reporting what has happened, analyzing contributing data to determine why it happened, and monitoring new data to determine what is happening now. Also known as *descriptive analytics* and *business intelligence*.

ROI   Return on investment

Rule   *See* Business rule.

S

SCIP   Strategy and change internal practice.

SCOR   Supply Chain Operations Reference

Scoring   The process of ranking alternatives according to their likelihood of being correct. Scoring is sometimes a step in predictive analytics.

SEE   Smarter enterprise enablement

Sentiment analysis   The process of analyzing social media data to determine opinion (positive or negative) on a topic. *See* Social media analytics; Text analytics.

SG&A   Sales, general, and administrative.

Simulation   The practice of building models based on experts' views on how the parts of a complicated system work.

SKU   Stock-keeping unit.

SMA   Social media analytics

Smarter enterprise   An enterprise that has optimized the entire system through the use of analytics, social media, mobile communications, and cloud technologies.

Social media analytics   The practice of "listening" to social media sources, such as Twitter or Facebook, and analyzing to determine the opinions, or sentiment, on a variety of topics.

SPC   Statistical Process Control

SPSS   Statistical Package for the Social Sciences

SSCA   Smarter Supply Chain Analytics

Statistical process control   A technique for detecting quality problems; it uses statistical methods and Western Electric decision rules for detecting "out-of-control" conditions on control charts.

STG   Systems and Technology Group

Structured data   Information (typically stored digitally) that either has a predefined data model or is organized in a predefined manner.

SWG   Software Group

Systems of engagement   Collaborative and sharing systems for consumers and employees that sometimes overlay tradition systems of record. Unlike systems of record, systems of engagement are unstructured and people-centric.

Systems of record   Traditional transaction systems that are structured and process-centric. *See also* Systems of engagement.

T

Text analytics   The practice of analyzing unstructured data.

Text matching   A computer program that looks for particular text.

TOP   Territory Optimization Program

Transactional data   Data produced by IT systems (typically known as systems of record) that run a business.

Transactional data store   The original source of transactional data.

Trusted data source   A source of data that has been verified to be correct and can be used with confidence.

U

UIMA   Unstructured Information Management Architecture

Univariate analysis   Statistical analysis done with the description of a single variable.

Unstructured data   Information (typically stored digitally) that either does not have a predefined data model or is not organized in a predefined manner. Most unstructured data is created by humans and includes email, documents, text messages, tweets, blogs, and more.

V

Variety   The forms of data, such as structured, text, and multimedia. One of the four Vs of big data.

Velocity   The speed at which data is available and the analysis of streaming data. One of the four Vs of big data.

Veracity   Data quality; managing the reliability of data. One of the four Vs of big data.

Volume   The size of data, which can range from terabytes to petabytes (or more). One of the four Vs of big data.

W-Z

Watson   The computer that triumphed in 2011 over two human champions in the quiz show *Jeopardy!* Also, it is the brand name for IBM's cognitive computing technology.

Index